Research-Based Reading Strategies in the Library for Adolescent Learners

Carianne Bernadowski, PhD
and
Patricia Liotta Kolencik, EdD

A LINWORTH PUBLISHING BOOK

LIBRARIES UNLIMITED
An Imprint of ABC-CLIO, LLC

ABC CLIO

Santa Barbara, California • Denver, Colorado • Oxford, England

Copyright 2010 by Libraries Unlimited

All rights reserved. No part of this publication may be reproduced, stored in a retrieval system, or transmitted, in any form or by any means, electronic, mechanical, photocopying, recording, or otherwise, except for the inclusion of brief quotations in a review, without prior permission in writing from the publisher.

Library of Congress Cataloging-in-Publication Data
Bernadowski, Carianne.
  Research-based reading strategies in the library for adolescent learners / Carianne Bernadowski and Patricia Kolencik.
    p. cm.
  "A Linworth Publishing book."
  Includes bibliographical references and index.
  ISBN-13: 978-1-58683-347-3 (pbk.)
  ISBN-10: 1-58683-347-2 (pbk.)
  1. Reading (Secondary) 2. Content area reading. 3. School libraries.
 I. Kolencik, Patricia Liotta. II. Title.
  LB1632.B47 2010
  428.4071'2—dc22   2009021198

ISBN: 978-1-58683-347-3
EISBN: 978-1-58683-404-3

14 13 12 11 10   1 2 3 4 5

This book is also available on the World Wide Web as an eBook.
Visit www.abc-clio.com for details.

ABC-CLIO, LLC
130 Cremona Drive, P.O. Box 1911
Santa Barbara, California 93116-1911

This book is printed on acid-free paper ∞

Manufactured in the United States of America

We dedicate this book to our families for their love
and support. Thank you for all that you do.

CONTENTS

Figures xiii
About the Authors xv
Introduction xvii
   NCTE/IRA Standards for English Language Arts xxi
   Information Literacy Standards for Student Learning xxiii
   Standards Alignment Chart xxv

PART I: COMPREHENSION STRATEGIES FOR THE LIBRARY AND CLASSROOM

1 Question-Answer Relationship 3
   Definition 3
   Research Findings 4
   Standards 6
   Strategy Nuts and Bolts: Implementation in the Library or Classroom 6
   Extending the Strategy for Diverse Learners and Students with Special Needs 11
   Collaborative Connections 11
   Assessment Tools 12
      Where Can I Learn More about Question-Answer Relationships? 15

	Web Extensions	15
	Works Cited	15
2	Think Alouds	17
	Definition	17
	Research Findings	17
	Standards	18
	Strategy Nuts and Bolts: Implementation in the Library or Classroom	18
	Extending the Strategy for Diverse Learners and Students with Special Needs	21
	Collaborative Connections	22
	Assessment Tools	22
	Where Can I Learn More about Think Alouds?	23
	Web Extensions	25
	Works Cited	25
3	Reciprocal Teaching	26
	Definition	26
	Research Findings	27
	Standards	27
	Strategy Nuts and Bolts: Implementation in the Library or Classroom	27
	Extending the Strategy for Diverse Learners and Students with Special Needs	30
	Collaborative Connections	31
	Assessment Tools	32
	Where Can I Learn More about Reciprocal Teaching?	32
	Web Extensions	32
	Works Cited	32
4	Anticipation Guides	35
	Definition	35
	Research Findings	36

	Standards	36
	Strategy Nuts and Bolts: Implementation in the Library or Classroom	36
	Extending the Strategy for Diverse Learners and Students with Special Needs	38
	Collaborative Connections	39
	Assessment Tools	39
	Where Can I Learn More about Anticipation Guides?	42
	Web Extensions	42
	Works Cited	42
5	Questioning the Author	43
	Definition	43
	Research Findings	44
	Standards	44
	Strategy Nuts and Bolts: Implementation in the Library or Classroom	44
	Extending the Strategy for Diverse Learners and Students with Special Needs	49
	Collaborative Connections	49
	Assessment Tools	51
	Where Can I Learn More about Questioning the Author?	51
	Web Extensions	54
	Works Cited	54
6	Survey, Question, Read, Recite, Review	55
	Definition	55
	Research Findings	55
	Standards	56
	Strategy Nuts and Bolts: Implementation in the Library or Classroom	56
	Extending the Strategy for Diverse Learners and Students with Special Needs	61
	Collaborative Connections	61

Assessment Tools	63
Where Can I Learn More about SQ3R?	63
Web Extensions	63
Works Cited	63

PART II: VOCABULARY STRATEGIES FOR THE LIBRARY AND CLASSROOM

7 Semantic Feature Analysis — 68

Definition	68
Research Findings	68
Standards	69
Strategy Nuts and Bolts: Implementation in the Library or Classroom	69
Extending the Strategy for Diverse Learners and Students with Special Needs	72
Collaborative Connections	74
Assessment Tools	74
Where Can I Learn More about Semantic Feature Analysis?	75
Web Extensions	75
Works Cited	75

8 Word Questioning Maps/Word Journals — 76

Definition	76
Research Findings	76
Standards	77
Strategy Nuts and Bolts: Implementation in the Library or Classroom	78
Word Questioning Map	79
Word Journals	81
Extending the Strategy for Diverse Learners and Students with Special Needs	82
Collaborative Connections	83
Assessment Tools	84
Where Can I Learn More about Word Questioning Maps/Word Journals?	84

	Web Extensions	85
	Works Cited	85
9	Frayer Model/Word Sorts	87
	Definition	87
	Research Findings	88
	Standards	88
	Strategy Nuts and Bolts: Implementation in the Library or Classroom	89
	Frayer Model	89
	Word Sorts	90
	Extending the Strategy for Diverse Learners and Students with Special Needs	95
	Collaborative Connections	96
	Assessment Tools	96
	Where Can I Learn More about Frayer Model/Word Sorts?	96
	Web Extensions	96
	Works Cited	98
Appendix: Collaboration: Web 2.0		*99*
Index		*107*

FIGURES

Figure SC1	Standards Alignment Chart	xxv
Figure 1.1	QAR	5
Figure 1.2	QAR Graphic Organizer	10
Figure 1.3	Question Brainstorming Web	13
Figure 1.4	QAR Class Tally Sheet	14
Figure 2.1	Think Aloud Self-Evaluation	20
Figure 2.2	Think Aloud Student Assessment Checklist	24
Figure 3.1	Reciprocal Teaching Organizer	29
Figure 3.2	Self-Assessment of Reciprocal Teaching	33
Figure 4.1	Anticipation Guide Template	37
Figure 4.2	Anticipation Guide Example	40
Figure 4.3	Anticipation Guide Self-Assessment	41
Figure 5.1	Query Tally Sheet	48
Figure 5.2	QtA Bookmark	50
Figure 5.3	Summary Evaluation Worksheet	52
Figure 6.1	SQ3R Chart	58
Figure 6.2	SQ3R Checklist	59

Figure 6.3 Herringbone/Fishbone Graphic Organizer   62

Figure 6.4 T-Chart   64

Figure 6.5 T-List   65

Figure 7.1 Semantic Feature Analysis Template   70

Figure 7.2 Semantic Feature Analysis Example   71

Figure 7.3 Information Retrieval Analysis Chart   73

Figure 8.1 Word Questioning Map   80

Figure 9.1 Frayer Model Graphic Organizer   91

Figure 9.2 Frayer Model Example   92

Figure 9.3 Word Sort Organizer   94

Figure 9.4 Keyword Search Expansion Chart   97

ABOUT THE AUTHORS

CARIANNE BERNADOWSKI, PhD, is an Assistant Professor of Elementary Education at Robert Morris University in Moon Township, Pennsylvania, in the School of Education and Social Sciences. She has taught elementary, secondary, and college students for the past 15 years. She holds a PhD from the University of Pittsburgh, in Pittsburgh, Pennsylvania, an MA in Reading Education from Slippery Rock University of Pennsylvania, in Slippery Rock, Pennsylvania, and a BA in Journalism and Communications/Secondary Education from Point Park College, in Pittsburgh. Currently, she teaches literacy courses at the undergraduate and graduate levels. She continues to work with school districts in the area of literacy. She has also coauthored a book for Linworth titled *Teaching with Books That Heal: Using Authentic Literacy and Literacy Strategies to Help Children Cope with Everyday Problems* and authored *Teaching Literacy Skills to Adolescents Using Coretta Scott King Award Winners* for Linworth Publishing, which was released October 31, 2009. She has written for *Library Media Connection, PA Reads, Reading Today, Teaching K-8, The Reading Professor,* and *Teaching Tolerance.*

When she is not writing or teaching, Dr. Bernadowski enjoys spending time with her sons, Maxwell and Liam, and her husband, Brian. She can be reached at bernadowski@rmu.edu.

PATRICIA LIOTTA KOLENCIK, EdD, is an associate professor in the Teacher Education Department at Clarion University of Pennsylvania, in Clarion. Prior to teaching at Clarion University, she was a high school librarian for 27 years. She holds a doctorate in Education from the University of Pittsburgh, in Pittsburgh, Pennsylvania, an MA from the University of Alabama, in Tuscaloosa, Alabama, and a BS.Ed. from Edinboro University of Pennsylvania, in Edinboro, Pennsylvania. Kolencik has authored numerous articles for various scholarly and professional journals, including *Library Media Connection*. She is the coauthor of Linworth's *Teaching with Books That Heal: Using Authentic Literature and Literacy Strategies to Help Children Cope with Everyday Problems* and has been a contributing author to Linworth's *Skills for Life*, 2nd edition. She can be reached at pkolencik@clarion.edu.

INTRODUCTION

"Every educator is a teacher of reading," as the expression goes. You may have a master's degree in library science or mathematics, but what do you really know about teaching reading? Who in the middle and high school helps students become more successful at reading narrative and expository text? The essential question then becomes, "Are you prepared to teach reading?" Many, if not all, librarians and educators are looking for ways to successfully incorporate content reading into their current curriculum. The content of this book aims to do just that.

Standards-based educational reform, school curricula, accountability measures, and demands of standardized tests require that all educators be held accountable for the success of all students. Much of that success stems from students being proficient and strategic readers and writers. It is estimated that approximately 8.7 million 4th- through 12th-grade students struggle with the reading and writing tasks that are required of them to perform in school (Kamil, 2003). This statistic clearly indicates that literacy instruction is a necessary component of middle and high school curricula across the nation. Likewise, this literacy instruction must come in the form of direct instruction (National Institute of Child Health and Human Development, 2007) that arms students with strategies to deal with unfamiliar and complicated text. However, many librarians and content-area teachers have limited training in content-area literacy pedagogy and are ill equipped when faced with students whose academic reading and writing skills are not aligned with their expectations (Strickland and Alvermann, 2004).

It is the authors' intention that literacy instruction be the shared responsibility of all departments at the secondary level, and librarians and teachers will find new and innovative ways to integrate reading and writing throughout the current curriculum. Research teaches us that good readers use many strategies simultaneously as they read, interpret, and interact with text. This text provides the librarian and the classroom teacher with researched-based instructional strategies to use before, during, and after reading to help even the best of readers, as well as those who struggle. Moreover, the librarian or the classroom teacher must be an active participant who models these strategies for students so they can eventually take ownership and use the strategies fluently and automatically. Finally, the librarian or the classroom teacher must be willing to provide a supportive instructional environment for students so that students can flourish and become proficient readers and writers.

A WORD ABOUT THE PURPOSE OF THE BOOK

This text, with its researched-based reading strategies, is designed to assist school librarians and classroom teachers as they strive to become teachers of reading. The authors are aware that school librarians and secondary classroom teachers receive limited pedagogical training in their professional preparation on the teaching of reading. It is our hope that this book will offer school librarians and classroom teachers additional pedagogical knowledge in the form of effective instructional best practices and researched-based strategies for teaching reading in a secondary school setting. The strategies in this book are designed so that librarians and classroom teachers can readily implement them in their daily practice to help students become comprehensive and strategic readers. We envision tweaks in the collaborative planning process between the librarian and the classroom teacher that will not only emphasize the development of reading skills but also push higher-level thinking skills into a position of prominence in the classroom and in the library so that students will become independent learners and critical users of information, thus, supporting the American Association of School Librarians (AASL) Standards for the 21st Century Learner.

Our motivation for writing *Research-Based Reading Strategies in the Library for Adolescent Learners* is to assist those who work with students in secondary education in implementing strategies that not only help students to read and to write proficiently but also engage them in learning the content that is so important to their understanding of themselves and their world—components of the framework for the Standards for the 21st Century Learner.

A WORD ABOUT THE INTENDED AUDIENCE

The primary audiences for this book are secondary school library media specialists and classroom teachers who work with grades 7 through 12, as well as other members of the learning community, such as literacy coaches, instructional support teachers, and Title I resource teachers who work with secondary students. Additionally, this book will be of value to those who home school at the secondary level.

A WORD ABOUT THE BOOK'S FORMAT

The book is divided into two major sections. Part I, consisting of six chapters, discusses a selection of researched-based reading comprehension strategies for use in the school library and the classroom. The following comprehension strategies are discussed in the chapters in Part I: Question Answer Relationships, Think Alouds, Reciprocal Teaching, Anticipation Guides, Questioning the Author, and SQ3R (Survey, Question, Read, Recite, Review).

Part II, which consists of three chapters, discusses a selection of researched-based vocabulary strategies that are essential to the reading process and to building a learner who can thrive in today's complex information environment. The vocabulary strategies discussed in Part II are Semantic Feature Analysis, Word Questioning Maps/Word Journals, and Frayer Model/Word Sorts.

Additionally, the book contains an appendix with references to Web 2.0 resources for both classroom teachers and librarians. There is also an index that includes all literacy strategies.

Each chapter contains:

- A definition of each instructional strategy
- The current research findings on the strategy
- The Information Literacy Standards for Student Learning and NCTE/IRA Standards for the English Language Arts
- The strategy's nuts and bolts
- Techniques for extending the strategy for diverse students and students with special needs

- Techniques for making collaborative connections with the classroom teacher
- Assessment tools
- Ready-to-go reproducibles
- A bibliography for finding additional information about the strategy
- Web extensions
- A Works Cited section

A WORD ABOUT THE SELECTION OF INSTRUCTIONAL STRATEGIES

The content in this book comes from a variety of resources that can be used by any educator who wants to learn more about how to teach secondary students to excel in reading. The resources include reviews of the research on reading instruction, reading methods textbooks, scholarly journal articles, and other resources on the teaching of reading.

The research in reading falls into four major categories: the text, the context of learning, the learners, and the learning strategies—all of which interact with each other. The authors of this text have selected instructional strategies for the teaching of reading on the basis of the aforementioned resources, the research of best practices for teaching and learning in America's schools, and their experience gathered in more than 30 years of teaching at the middle level and in secondary education. It is the authors' fervent hope that these strategies will enhance your daily instruction by engaging students more actively in the reading process to develop lifelong learning skills that promote personal growth, enjoyment, and new understandings for now and in the future.

Each chapter has a section titled "Extending the Strategy for Diverse Students and Students with Special Needs." The purpose of this section is to provide successful reading techniques to help these diverse, struggling readers become proficient.

Each chapter also has a section entitled "Collaborative Connections," which describes a shared planning and teaching process for the librarian and the classroom teacher to partner to teach each strategy. It is the authors' hope that librarians and classroom teachers will find this section noteworthy because it provides effective approaches to blend reading strategies with critical information literacy skills, thus making for total packaging to address the Information Literacy Standards for Student Learning, the Standards for the English Language Arts, and the Standards for the 21st Century Learner. The authors believe that librarians and teachers together face the challenge of and share joint responsibility for facilitating the development of both formal and informal reading comprehension skills because reading is the basic tool through which students become independent learners and critical consumers of information. The classroom teacher and the librarian, functioning as a team, share the responsibility for designing and implementing a program that not only addresses the standards but also supports lifelong learning. Because of the magnitude of the demands made in today's educational environment with regard to accountability, the authors designed the "Collaborative Connections" sections within the chapters of this book to draw upon the shared competencies of the librarian and the classroom teacher.

Each chapter concludes with a bibliography of resources for librarians and classroom teachers who wish to learn more about the chapter's strategy, a section on Web site connections and extensions, and a reference section specifying works consulted on the chapter's strategy.

Works Cited

Kamil, Michael. *Adolescents and Literacy: Reading for the 21st Century.* Washington, DC: Alliance for Excellent Education, 2003.
National Institute of Child Health and Human Development. *What Content-Area Teachers Should Know about Adolescent Literacy.* Washington, DC: U.S. Government Printing Office, 2007.
Strickland, Dorothy, and Susan D. Alvermann. "Learning and Teaching Literacy in Grades 4–12: Issues and Challenges." In D. S. Strickland and D. E. Alvermann (Eds.), *Bridging the Literacy Achievement Gap, Grades 4–12.* New York: Teachers College Press, 2004.

NCTE/ IRA STANDARDS FOR ENGLISH LANGUAGE ARTS

1. Students read a wide range of print and non-print texts to build an understanding of texts, of themselves, and of the cultures of the United States and the world; to acquire new information; to respond to the needs and demands of society and the workplace; and for personal fulfillment. Among

these texts are fiction and nonfiction, classic and contemporary works.
2. Students read a wide range of literature from many periods in many genres to build an understanding of the many dimensions (e.g., philosophical, ethical, aesthetic) of human experience.
3. Students apply a wide range of strategies to comprehend, interpret, evaluate, and appreciate texts. They draw on their prior experience, their interactions with other readers and writers, their knowledge of word meaning and of other texts, their word identification strategies, and their understanding of textual features (e.g., sound-letter correspondence, sentence structure, context, graphics).
4. Students adjust their use of spoken, written, and visual language (e.g., conventions, style, vocabulary) to communicate effectively with a variety of audiences and for different purposes.
5. Students employ a wide range of strategies as they write and use different writing process elements appropriately to communicate with different audiences for a variety of purposes.
6. Students apply knowledge of language structure, language conventions (e.g., spelling and punctuation), media techniques, figurative language, and genre to create, critique, and discuss print and non-print texts.
7. Students conduct research on issues and interests by generating ideas and questions, and by posing problems. They gather, evaluate, and synthesize data from a variety of sources (e.g., print and non-print texts, artifacts, people) to communicate their discoveries in ways that suit their purpose and audience.
8. Students use a variety of technological and information resources (e.g., libraries, databases, computer networks, video) to gather and synthesize information and to create and communicate knowledge.
9. Students develop an understanding of and respect for diversity in language use, patterns, and dialects across cultures, ethnic groups, geographic regions, and social roles.
10. Students whose first language is not English make use of their first language to develop competency in the English

language arts and to develop understanding of content across the curriculum.
11. Students participate as knowledgeable, reflective, creative, and critical members of a variety of literacy communities.
12. Students use spoken, written, and visual language to accomplish their own purposes (e.g., for learning, enjoyment, persuasion, and the exchange of information)

Standards for the English Language Arts, by the International Reading Association and National Council for Teachers of English, Copyright 1996 by the International Reading Association and the National Council for Teachers of English. Reprinted with permission.

INFORMATION LITERACY STANDARDS FOR STUDENT LEARNING

Information Literacy

Standard 1: The student who is information literate accesses information efficiently and effectively.

Standard 2: The student who is information literate evaluates information critically and competently.

Standard 3: The student who is information literate uses information accurately and creatively.

Independent Learning

Standard 4: The student who is an independent learner is information literate and pursues information related to personal interests.

Standard 5: The student who is an independent learner is information literate and appreciates literature and other creative expressions of information.

Standard 6: The student who is an independent learner is information literate and strives for excellence in information seeking and knowledge generation.

Social Responsibility

Standard 7: The student who contributes positively to the learning community and to society is information literate and recognizes the importance of information to a democratic society.

Standard 8: The student who contributes positively to the learning community and to society is information literate and practices ethical behavior in regard to information and information technology.

Standard 9: The student who contributes positively to the learning community and to society is information literate and participates effectively in groups to pursue and generate information.

Information Literacy Standards for Student Learning, by the American Library Association and the Association for Educational Communications and Technology. Copyright 1998. Reprinted with permission from the American Library Association.

The Standards Alignment Chart presented in Figure SC1 will help the librarian and the classroom teacher make the necessary connection to standards-based education. Each strategy is listed with applicable national standards as listed above.

Chapter and Title	Information Literacy Standards for Student Learning	NCTE/IRA Standards for the English Language Arts
Chapter 1: Question-Answer Relationships	3,6	3,7,11,12
Chapter 2: Think Alouds	2,3,4,5,6	3,7,11,12
Chapter 3: Reciprocal Teaching	2,3,4,5,6	1,3,5,7,8,10,11,12
Chapter 4: Anticipation Guides	2,3,4,5,6	1,3,5,7,8,10,11,12
Chapter 5: Questioning the Author	2,3,4,5,6	3,7,11,12
Chapter 6: SQ3R	2,3,4,5,6	3,7,11,12
Chapter 7: Semantic Feature Analysis	2,3,4,5	1,3,4,7,8,11,12
Chapter 8: Word Questioning Maps/Word Journals	1,2,3,6	1,2,4,5,6,8,9,11,12
Chapter 9: Frayer Model/ Word Sorts	1, 2, 3, 6	1, 2,4,5,6,8,9,11,12

FIGURE SC1: Standards Alignment Chart

PART I

Comprehension Strategies for the Library and Classroom

1

Question-Answer Relationship

DEFINITION

The Question-Answer Relationship (QAR) strategy, developed by Taffy Raphael, is a student-centered questioning technique that teaches readers to categorize questions according to where they would find the answers. Since teachers rely primarily on questioning to check for comprehension (Durkin, 1978), it is imperative that students know where to find the information to answer such questions. This strategy is valuable for helping readers realize the need to consider both the text and their background knowledge when reading and comprehending text. "QAR is a comprehension strategy that provides a way to think and talk about sources of information for answering questions" (Raphael, Highfield, and Au, 2006). QAR requires teachers and librarians to explicitly model the types of questions typically asked by teachers and tests, even standardized test questions (Raphael and Au, 2005). QAR is a reflective process that gives students the tools to recognize the relationship between questions teachers ask, the answers they expect, and questions commonly found on standardized tests. The ultimate goal of this strategy is for students to eventually begin to develop and generate their own questions when reading. Students often use a literal approach to answering questions, unaware of the various levels of thinking (Buehl, 2001) required to truly comprehend text and to answer questions pertaining to text. Additionally, the QAR strategy gives teachers and students a common language for discussion about text and questions pertaining to text. Moreover, the QAR strategy provides a solid foundation for the five-step I-Search research process.

QAR relationships consist of four types of questions: *Right There, Think and Search, Author and You,* and *On Your Own* (Raphael, 1982, 1984, 1986). It is recommended that classroom teachers and/or librarians introduce each type of question individually "so that students can deepen their understanding of each before moving onto a new type of question" (Fisher et al., 2006). Figure 1.1 is a visual representation of the types of questions. This can be used as a handout for students or for environmental posters.

RESEARCH FINDINGS

- QAR was designed to be taught and learned using a wide variety of texts (Raphael, Highfield, and Au, 2006).
- The QAR strategy is accessible to students with diverse backgrounds, ages, and ability levels (Raphael, Highfield, and Au, 2006).
- Students who learned and practiced this strategy for as little as eight weeks showed significant gains in reading comprehension (Richardson and Morgan, 1994).
- Current studies demonstrate that when students experience explicit instruction of comprehension strategies, it improves their comprehension of new texts and topics (Hiebert et al., 1998).
- No comprehension activity has a longer or more pervasive tradition than asking students questions about their reading, whether this occurs before, during, or after reading (Duke and Pearson, 2002).
- A student's understanding and recall can be readily shaped by the types of questions to which the student becomes accustomed (Duke and Pearson, 2002).
- Questioning is effective for improving comprehension because it gives the students a purpose for reading, focuses attention on what must be learned, helps develop active thinking while reading, helps monitor comprehension, helps review content, and relates what is learned to what is already known (Armbruster et al., 2001).

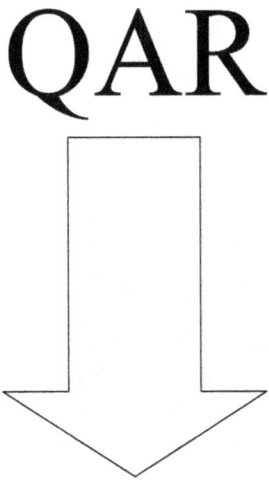
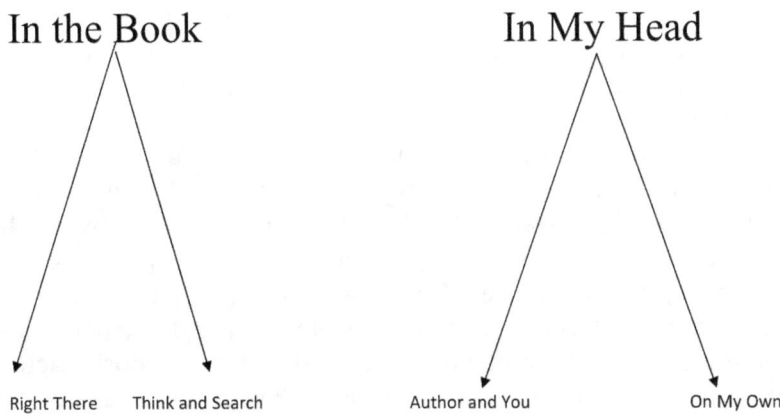

FIGURE 1.1: QAR

- Teacher questioning strongly supports and advances students' learning from reading (Armbruster et al., 2001).

STANDARDS

Information Literacy Standards: 3,6
NCTE/IRA Standards for the English Language Arts: 3,7,11,12

STRATEGY NUTS AND BOLTS: IMPLEMENTATION IN THE LIBRARY OR CLASSROOM

Question-Answer Relationship (QAR) not only requires students to be aware of the types of questions that exist but also requires the librarian or classroom teacher to model questions that include explicit instruction, modeling/thinking aloud, scaffolding, coaching, and independent practice. QAR helps students realize the need to consider both information in the text and information from their own background knowledge (Raphael, 1986).

QAR encourages students to engage with text by asking and answering questions. QAR discourages students from overreliance on text and encourages them to make connections by locating information, determining text structures, and making inferences—three valuable comprehension strategies vital to becoming a competent, skilled reader. Initially, students learn to use text information combined with their knowledge base and experiences to answer questions. Finally, the strategy teaches children to "read between the lines" in order to answer questions about text by making accurate and appropriate inferences. Throughout each phase of instruction, the librarian or classroom teacher gradually releases the responsibility of the strategy to the students. It is essential that classroom teachers and librarians collaborate and navigate through this process. With that said, the QAR strategy is time consuming and takes patience to implement in any setting. It might be helpful for the librarian and the classroom teacher to share the responsibility of teaching this strategy, that is, to co-teach the lesson. Once most students have mastered a category of questions, the teacher and the librarian can then work with students who may be struggling with a particular question type.

The following steps can be used as a framework for teaching students to use QAR with text:

(Steps 1 and 2 Should Be Modeled for Students Using a Reader-Friendly Short Text So that Students Can Concentrate on the Strategy Implementation.)

1. The librarian or classroom teacher begins by explaining to students the two broad categories of questions that are referred to as *In the Book* and *In My Head*. The *In the Book* category consists of text-based questions. This category consists of two types of question: *Right There* questions and *Think and Search* questions. A *Right There* question is one in which the answer can be found directly in the text in a single sentence. The second type of *In the Book* question is called a *Think and Search*. A *Think and Search* question requires students to find the answer by making connections within and inferences from the text. The answer can be found in several places in the text, such as across sentences, pages, paragraphs, and/or texts (Raphael, Highfield, and Au, 2006). The librarian or classroom teacher should provide many examples of each type of question before moving to step two. Extensive modeling and practice are recommended in order for students to learn to recognize the two types of *In the Book* questions. As collaborative partners, the classroom teacher and the librarian might find it helpful to use a team-teaching approach during this phase of instruction. Students need help in the form of scaffolding, as well as guidance in developing a schema for organizing and categorizing information as they begin the research process. By explicitly "walking" them through the process by using the QAR strategy, the instructors help the students become better equipped to transform raw information into a quality research product.

2. Next, the librarian or classroom teacher introduces students to the category of *In My Head* questions that consists of *Author and Me* and *On My Own* questions. An *Author and Me* question requires students to use information from the text coupled with their own background knowledge. In other words, the answer cannot be found in the text, yet the reader must think about how the text and her own knowledge fit together in order to answer the question. The second *In My Head* question is called *On My Own*. In this

type of question, the reader does not need the text to answer the question. Readers must rely on their own experience and/or knowledge to answer the question. *On My Own* questions can be used prior to reading a text to activate and access the reader's background knowledge and set a purpose for reading.

3. The librarian or classroom teacher should provide many examples of each type of question before moving to step three. Extensive modeling and practice are recommended in order for students to learn to recognize the two types of *In my Head* questions. A special place in the library media center, such as a bulletin board or wall to display the types of questions, can be helpful. This gives students a visual reference to use and accessibility to the information while they are learning the QAR strategy.

4. Choose a text with several paragraphs, and place on transparency or document camera. Then distribute the QAR Graphic Organizer in Figure 1.2 to students. Students write the question and answer in the appropriate section as the whole class follows along on the transparency or document camera. It is important to model slowly for students. Students may need extended guided practice. This extended guided practice can be easily handled by the classroom teacher if the two instructors are working collaboratively. The librarian may work with a small group in a similar manner.

5. Read the selection aloud, with students stopping at predetermined sections to ask the four types of questions—*Right There, Think and Search, Author and You,* and *On My Own.*

6. Students write the question in the appropriate section and answer in parentheses. It is important that students verbalize where they found the information. For *Right There* and *Think and Search* questions, the librarian or classroom teacher can underline or circle information on the transparency so that students can see where the information was found in the text.

7. After several modeling sessions, allow students to develop their own questions from text selections chosen by the librarian or classroom teacher.

8. Students can work in groups to find answers to questions and develop their own questions.

QAR does not have to be used exclusively with text. The same principles can be applied to text supports such as graphs, charts, and photographs. Web sites, wikis, and blogs are acceptable alternatives.

The following is a list of QAR questions that might be asked during a unit on magnetism:

Right There Questions

What attracts a magnet?

Think and Search

What is the difference between a natural magnet and an artificial magnet?

Author and You Questions

What types of magnets would you use in your school locker or on your refrigerator door?

On My Own Questions

Did you ever find a magnetic rock?
What items do I have in my home that use electricity?

Classroom teachers and librarians work together to help students successfully understand and apply the QAR strategy. Successful collaboration can be achieved if the librarian supports the classroom teacher by teaching one of the four types of questions. Let us think of the QAR strategy from the librarian's role in the teaching of the research process. The QAR strategy forms the scaffolding of the entire research process. It is that integral part of the research process that assists students in developing thoughtful, essential questions needed to move from topic to thesis in the research process. As all librarians have experienced, students collect all that great information from all those fabulous sources and then falter. Students need help in the form of scaffolding that this strategy provides. Thus, this strategy provides practice and application in a technique that will guide students toward developing the "meatier" essential questions that inspire critical thought and that are worth their research time and energy. Librarians and teachers can confer with students to help them select the most promising questions to research. In sum, the QAR strategy develops skills and competencies for independent research, and the coaching role of the librarian in the planning and teaching of questioning strategies with the classroom teacher is vital.

In the Text Questions	In My Head Questions
Right There	Author and You
Think and Search	On My Own

FIGURE 1.2: QAR Graphic Organizer

EXTENDING THE STRATEGY FOR DIVERSE LEARNERS AND STUDENTS WITH SPECIAL NEEDS

The Question-Answer Relationship (QAR) strategy has improved the reading comprehension of students in a variety of geographical and educational settings, including suburban and rural schools and in both general education and bilingual education. Since this strategy is a process and takes much time and practice to master, modification for English Language Learners and students with special needs can be easily implemented. Extended practice time with each type of question allows students to fully understand and practice each category. Linda Darling-Hammond (1995) found that students with diverse backgrounds tend to receive a great deal of instruction in low-level skills but little to no instruction in comprehension. QAR is easily accessible to all students through its easy-to-understand language and the visual representation made using a graphic organizer. Further modifications can be made by giving students bookmarks with the four types of questions for easy reference. Wall charts and posters can make a great addition to the classroom or library and provide immediate environmental support for these students. Furthermore, carefully introducing the types of questions slowly is of optimal benefit. Diverse learners may need extended time to distinguish between *In the Book* and *In My Head* questions.

COLLABORATIVE CONNECTIONS

Classroom teachers rely on the librarian to be the expert in the media center. Working together for a common goal can help students be successful readers and writers. QAR naturally allows this opportunity for classroom teachers and librarians to work as a team to teach students to interact with the text. The classroom teacher and the librarian can work together to choose the reading materials on many levels as well as to help students construct questions that lead to higher-level learning. Although students do not generally engage in a formal reading lesson while visiting the media center, students do learn much about literacy incidentally, without direct intention. While working with students, librarians can teach students that authors, tests, and teachers generally ask four types of questions, and these four types of questions are presented in the QAR strategy. Graphic organizers are easy-to-use visual learning tools that can help students categorize their own questions while engaged in research. Distribution of the graphic organizer to students can help support teachers as they work with this strategy in their classrooms. Furthermore, the librarian can support the teacher by displaying the types of questions on bulletin boards or other highly visible areas in the library media center. Finally, QAR question categories can be easily integrated into inquiry-based learning. For example, while students are researching, teachers can require them to use the four types of questions to guide them in their pursuit of information. This strategy teaches students that questioning does not stop with the initial or main question. The role of the library media specialist is to guide students and to encourage them to continue to ask questions throughout the information search process. The strategy teaches students to identify questions, making students more enthusiastic when it comes to seeking answers, answers that are not given facts but that must be constructed from the information that is found. In sum, the QAR is a connection-building strategy to help students understand content; thus, successful research projects are dependent on the quality of the questions. As part of the research process and to extend this strategy once students have a solid background to think and wonder about, librarians and classroom teachers could use a Question Brainstorming Web like the one found in Figure 1.3 to help students continue to develop effective questions to guide their research. Helping students to become more conscious of the kinds of questions they formulate will result in the generation of higher-level thinking skills.

ASSESSMENT TOOLS

The goal of the QAR strategy is to successfully teach students how to ask and answer questions using text and their background knowledge. As you work with students on mastering the four types of questions, you want to ensure that each student is working toward mastery of the strategy. A class tally sheet is one way to keep track of each student's progress. Each time students are required to use the strategy and the QAR Graphic Organizer in Figure 1.2, the librarian or classroom teacher can keep a record of their progress using the Class Tally Sheet in Figure 1.4. Assessment can be completed informally by using anecdotal records and student observations. Students can also write journal entries explaining the QAR strategy and the process they used while engaged in the strategy, a metacognitive approach. If

Directions: Choose a topic and write it in the center scroll. Record questions you have about the topic in the surrounding scrolls. Continue to refine your questions as you further explore the topic.

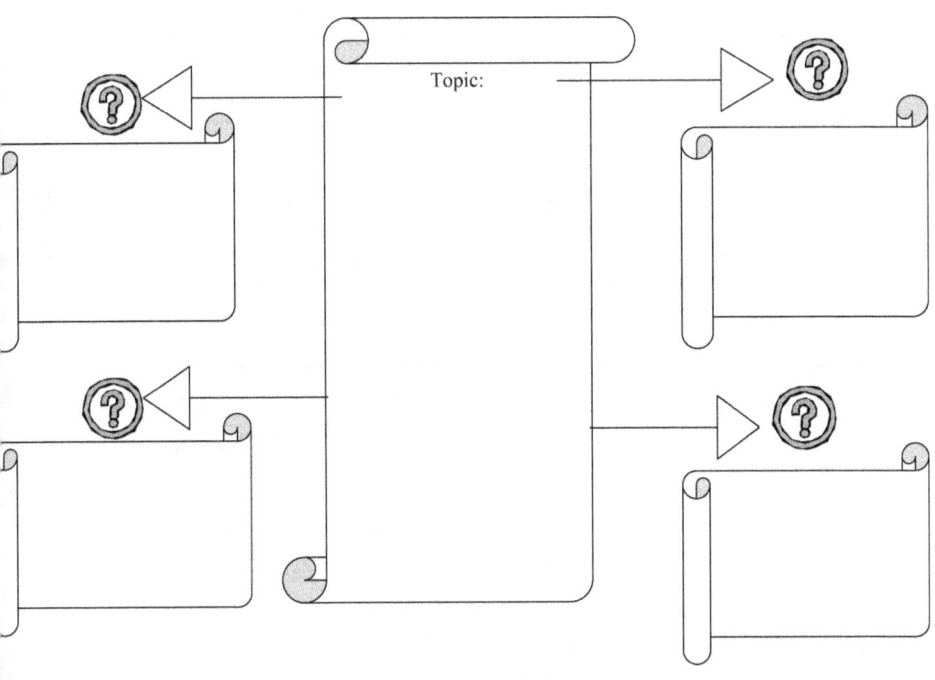

List two questions you would like to explore for your research project.
1.

2.

FIGURE 1.3: Question Brainstorming Web

Date: _____   Text: _____

Name of Student	Number of Questions for QAR Answered Correctly
Ex: Jim Jones	5/6

FIGURE 1.4: QAR Class Tally Sheet

students are writing in a journal, teachers can require students to answer how and why the strategy was helpful in their comprehension of that particular text.

Where Can I Learn More about Question-Answer Relationships?

Billmeyer, Rachel, and Mary Lee Baron. *Teaching Reading in the Content Areas: If Not Me, Then Who?* Aurora, CO: Mid-Continent Research for Education & Learning, 1998.

McIntosh, Margaret E., and Roni Jo Draper. "Using the Question-Answer Relationship Strategy to Improve Students' Reading of Mathematics Texts." *The Clearing House* (Jan.-Feb. 1996): 154–162.

Pearson, P. David, and Dale D. Johnson. *Teaching Reading Comprehension.* New York: Holt, Rinehart, & Winston, 1978.

Web Extensions

<http://www.readwritethink.org/lessons/lesson_view.asp?id=370>
<http://www.teachervision.fen.com/lesson-plan/reading-comprehension/48701.html>
<http://www.associatedcontent.com/article/321987/lesson_plan_question_and_answer_relationships.html>
<http://www.readingquest.org/strat/qar.html>

Works Cited

Armbruster, Bonnie B., et al. *Put Reading First: The Research Building Blocks for Teaching Children to Read.* Washington, DC: U.S Department of Education, 2001.

Buehl, Doug. *Classroom Strategies for Interactive Learning.* 2nd ed. Newark, DE: International Reading Association, 2001.

Darling-Hammond, Linda. "Changing Conceptions of Teaching and Teacher Development." *Teacher Education Quarterly* (1995): 9–26.

Duke, Nell, and P. David Pearson. "Effective Practices for Developing Reading Comprehension." In A. Farstrup and S. Samuels (Eds.), *What Research Has to Say about Reading Instruction.* Newark, DE: International Reading Association, 2002, pp. 205–242.

Durkin, Dolores. "What Classroom Observation Reveals about Reading Comprehension Instruction." *Reading Research Quarterly* 14 (1978): 481–533.

Fisher, Douglas, et al. *50 Content Area Strategies for Adolescent Literacy.* Upper Saddle River, NJ: Pearson, 2006.

Hiebert, Elfrieda H., et al. *Every Child a Reader.* Ann Arbor, MI: Center for the Improvement of Early Reading Achievement, 1998.

Raphael, Taffy E. "Teaching Children Question-Answering Strategies." *The Reading Teacher* 36 (1982): 186–191.

Raphael, Taffy E. "Teaching Learners about Sources of Information for Answering Questions." *Journal of Reading* 27 (1984): 303–311.

Raphael, Taffy E. "Teaching Children Question-Answering Relationships, Revisited." *The Reading Teacher* 39 (1986): 516–522.

Raphael, Taffy, and Kathryn Au. "QAR: Enhancing Comprehension and Test Taking across Grade and Content Areas." *The Reading Teacher* 59 (2005): 206–221.

Raphael, Taffy, Kathy Highfield, and Kathryn Au. *QAR Now: A Powerful and Practical Framework That Develops Comprehension and Higher-Level Thinking in All Students.* New York: Scholastic, 2006.

Richardson, Judy S., and Raymond F. Morgan. *Reading to Learn in the Content Areas.* Belmont, CA: Wadsworth, 1994.

2

Think Alouds

DEFINITION

A think aloud is an instructional strategy to help students improve reading comprehension by verbalizing metacognitive strategies while reading text. By watching others model what good readers do when faced with confusing or difficult text, students can learn what expert readers do when confronted with challenging reading, thus learning how the mind works in this situation. Think alouds are highly recommended to help students improve their reading comprehension and metacognitive processes. Furthermore, they are the only reading comprehension strategy that allows teachers, librarians, or other observers to see and hear what goes on in the mind of the reader. The think aloud strategy includes self-questioning and knowing how to find answers; visualizing; retelling in order to understand; predicting, reading, and verifying; rereading and reading on; and inferring. This strategy is implemented by modeling how a good reader thinks through what is being read, stops at intervals, thinks about how the text is being understood, and uses self-talk.

RESEARCH FINDINGS

The think aloud strategy requires students to verbalize their thoughts while reading, thus revealing their hidden insights and/or misunderstandings. The think aloud can be a valuable strategy for individual or small- or whole-group implementation. This strategy can also be used as an informal or formal assessment tool as the librarian and the teacher check for comprehension. Furthermore, this metacognitive strategy gives librarians or classroom teachers insights into students' reading processing strategies by listening to what the students say during the think aloud.

- Think alouds are effective as a diagnostic tool to assess students' abilities to use inferences as they read (Laing and Kamhi, 2002).
- Students who verbalize their thoughts while reading score significantly higher on comprehension tests (Anderson and Roit, 1993).
- Think alouds are effective as directed reading-thinking activities in teaching the skill of comprehension monitoring (Baumann, Seifert-Kessell, and Jones, 1992.)
- Think alouds use a modeling technique to help students improve their comprehension (Davey, 1983).

STANDARDS

Information Literacy Standards: 2,3,4,5,6
NCTE/IRA Standards for the English Language Arts: 3,7,11,12

STRATEGY NUTS AND BOLTS: IMPLEMENTATION IN THE LIBRARY OR CLASSROOM

Tierney, Readence, and Dishner (1995) suggest five goals to include in the think aloud process and indicate that each of these key words specifies strategies good readers use as they read. The key words are:

- Picture
- Predict
- "Like a"
- Problem
- Fix up

For example, proficient readers picture a scene in their head, predict what will happen next, compare text structures to each other, recognize problems in comprehension, and apply "fix-up" strategies such as rereading. These skills and processes can be targeted as students work in the library media center on the research process or other inquiry-based projects.

The following steps are used to implement the think aloud:

1. Librarians or classroom teachers choose a passage that contains unfamiliar words or confusing parts so that the librarian or teacher can model how to deal with confusion while reading. The students should have a copy of the text and read along silently with the librarian or classroom teacher as he reads aloud. The text can be any text, either from a book or in an electronic format. For example, in the media center, the librarian may use a blog or Internet article to model the think aloud. The librarian may find this strategy helpful when working with individuals students during the research process.
2. Librarians or classroom teachers model the strategy by reading the text aloud and stopping periodically to verbalize what is going on in their mind while reading. While the librarian or classroom teacher is reading, students read silently and listen carefully to what the instructor is doing. Students can take notes as well, either in the margins or on sticky notes.
3. Librarians or classroom teachers verbalize their thoughts as they read aloud by modeling the kinds of strategies a skilled reader uses during reading. One useful strategy is to read and ask oneself if the reading "makes sense," which models comprehension monitoring for students. Additionally, predicting and verifying, asking questions, rereading, and making inferences are strategies that must be explicitly demonstrated for students.
4. Librarians or classroom teachers model how to conduct a think aloud as students follow along silently. The librarian or classroom teacher can use the following to help with this process.
   A. Make predictions before and during reading and show students how to develop hypotheses by saying "I think . . . will happen next," or revise and/or confirm predictions by stating, "That prediction was true because the text states . . ."
   B. Help students create visual images in their mind by stating, "This made me think of . . ." or "I can see that. . . ."

Name: _____

	Not Often	Sometimes	Often
I form mind pictures (visualize).			
I make predictions.			
I confirm/revise my predictions.			
I use comparisons.			
I monitor my comprehension and use fix-up strategies.			
I use context clues to figure out unfamiliar words in the text.			
I use my background knowledge to make sense of the text.			

FIGURE 2.1: Think Aloud Self-Evaluation

C. Share an analogy with students or model how prior knowledge and experiences apply by stating, "This is like the time. . . ."
D. Verbalize a confusing part or show how you monitor your own comprehension. Statements such as "That doesn't make sense," "I'm confused by . . . ," or "I wonder why . . ." demonstrate for students what expert readers do when faced with reading difficulty.
E. Demonstrate appropriate fix-up strategies for students. Statement like "I am not sure how this fits into what I've already learned," "This is not what I expected," "Maybe I should reread that part," and "I need to think about this" show students the need to monitor comprehension and implement a fix-up strategy to improve comprehension.

5. Students then read the next section with expert supervision, thinking aloud and talking about the strategies they used while reading the text. The librarian or classroom teacher gradually turns over the responsibility to the students to practice the strategy, taking turns in oral reading.
6. The students can then be given the Think Aloud Self Assessment Checklist in Figure 2.1 to self-evaluate their progress and/or a partner's progress.

EXTENDING THE STRATEGY FOR DIVERSE LEARNERS AND STUDENTS WITH SPECIAL NEEDS

Teaching diverse learners how to use the think aloud while reading is valuable because it puts words to the process of reading: reading with a voice. Rarely do librarians or classroom teachers have the opportunity to find out what goes on in the mind of a reader; think alouds give instructors that luxury. When working with English Language Learners (ELL), it is critical that librarians and classroom teachers keep in mind that second language development occurs in stages, advancing from silent and receptive. These students can understand some words but may not be comfortable speaking them. Since librarians and classroom teachers are modeling the process, their guidance is essential to this strategy. Additionally, repetition and extended guidance are recommended when working with students with special needs or with ELL students. Finally, allowing students to work with a peer who demonstrates good comprehension abilities can provide the support a diverse learner needs. Suggesting that students verbalize and write their questions on a copy of the text is also beneficial. Other suggestions include making a T-chart or keeping a learning log on what students have read, viewed, or heard. Moreover, the diverse learner or the learner with special needs benefits from repeating the steps in the process.

COLLABORATIVE CONNECTIONS

Typically, the classroom teacher models this strategy for students in the classroom over a period of time. The librarian can successfully support students while working in the library media center. For example, when students are conducting research on a topic such as cloning, the librarian may find opportunities to help students think through their processing of information from a book or electronic text. If a student is confused about information found in a source, librarians can model for students how they process the information. This modeling is done orally so that students can hear the metacognitive process. The librarian simply reads a portion of the text aloud and models the think aloud. This gives students the tools they need to replicate such a strategy when reading and researching independently.

As students continue their research, they may be confronted with difficult or confusing text and/or information. The librarian can easily conduct an impromptu think aloud to help students process information more coherently and easily.

ASSESSMENT TOOLS

Lytle (1982) suggests that six categories of statements are made during the think aloud process: (1) Monitoring of doubts (I don't understand); (2) signaling understanding (Now, I understand why); (3) analysis of text features (This is a cause and effect because . . . I); (4) elaboration of the text (I think of . . . when I read this); (5) judgments of the text (I like when the author . . .); and (6) reasoning (I know this because . . .).

Thus, the librarian or classroom teacher should consider the following questions as a means of assessing a think aloud lesson:

- Does the reader use background/prior knowledge to link with new learning in order to make meaning?
- Is the reader able to describe what is being visualized as reading takes place?
- Does the reader know when to use appropriate "fix-up" strategies to monitor comprehension?
- Does the reader self-monitor and self-correct while reading?
- Can the reader explain or defend predictions and confirmations?
- Does the reader use context clues and/or background knowledge to deal with unfamiliar vocabulary?
- Does the reader use text structure knowledge to aid in comprehension?

The Think Aloud Student Assessment Checklist in Figure 2.2 can be used to assess each student individually. Although the librarian may not deliver a formal reading lesson, it may be helpful to review the assessment checklist for skills that students need in order to be successful with this process to improve comprehension. Additionally, the librarian can be a key player in working with ELL/ESL students by paying special attention to the tone of feedback given to these students and by finding a sampling of resources in print, on the Web, in databases, or in a video to support these students.

Where Can I Learn More about Think Alouds?

Irwin, Judith W. *Teaching Reading Comprehension Processes*. 3rd ed. Boston: Pearson, 2007.

Lapp, D., et al. "You Can Read This Text—I'll Show You How: Interactive Comprehension instruction." *Journal of Adolescent and Adult Literacy* (2008): 372–381.

McKenna, Michael C., and Richard D. Robinson. *Teaching through text: A Content Literacy Approach to Content Area Reading*. White Plains, NY: Longman, 1993.

Rhodes, Lynn K., and Nancy Shanklin. *Windows into Literacy*. Portsmouth, NH: Heinemann, 1993.

Vacca, Jo Ann, et al. *Reading and Learning to Read*. 6th ed. New York: Allyn & Bacon, 2006.

Name: _____ Date: _____

_____ The reader understands his purposes for reading.

Observations:

_____ The reader verbalizes when she creates visual images while reading.

Observations:

_____ The reader makes predictions before, during, and after reading.

Observations:

_____ The reader confirms and/or revises predictions during and after reading.

Observations:

_____ The reader uses context clues to figure out unfamiliar vocabulary while reading.

Observations:

_____ The reader provides verbal evidence of comprehension monitoring.

Observations:

_____ The reader provides verbal evidence of application of fix-up strategies.

Observations:

FIGURE 2.2: Think Aloud Student Assessment Checklist

Wade, Susan E. "Using Think Alouds to Assess Comprehension." *The Reading Teacher* (March 1990): 442–451.

Web Extensions

<http://www.brighthub.com/education/k-12/articles/6734.aspx>
<http://www.teachervision.fen.com/skill-builder/problem-solving/48546.html>
<http://teachers.net/lessonplans/posts/1237.html>
<http://www.readwritethink.org/lesson_images/lesson212/thinkaloud.pdf>

Works Cited

Anderson, Valerie, and Marsha Roit. "Planning and Implementing Collaborative Strategy Instruction for Delayed Readers in Grades 6–10." *Elementary School Journal* (November 1993): 121–137.

Baumann, James F., Nancy Seifert-Kessell, and, Leah. A. Jones. "Using Think Alouds to Enhance Children's Comprehension Monitoring Abilities." *The Reading Teacher* (November 1993): 184–193.

Davey, Beth. (1983). "Think Aloud: Modeling the Cognitive Processes of Reading Comprehension." *Journal of Reading* (October 1983): 44–47.

Laing, Sandra P., and Alan G. Kamhi. "The Use of Think-Aloud Protocols to Compare Inferencing Abilities in Average and Below-Average Readers." *Journal of Learning Disabilities* (September 2002): 437–448.

Lytle, Susan. L. "Exploring Comprehension Style: A Study of Twelfth Grade Readers' Transactions with Text." Doctoral Dissertation, University of Pennsylvania. *Dissertation Abstracts International* 43: 2295A.

Tierney, Robert J., et al. *Reading Strategies and Practices: A Compendium.* 6th ed. Boston: Pearson-Allyn & Bacon, 2005.

3

Reciprocal Teaching

DEFINITION

Reciprocal teaching is an interactive instructional questioning strategy that encourages students to ask informed questions and promotes independent learning from a text through inquiry and dialogue. Reciprocal teaching has four components: prediction, summarization, questioning, and clarification. Based on the work of Palincsar and Brown (1986), it is designed to have students "take on" the role of the teacher by generating questions from their reading to bring meaning to the text. This strategy provides a simple introduction to group discussion techniques aimed at understanding, remembering, and analyzing text content though questioning. It is a highly structured metacognitive method that incorporates a number of language arts—listening, writing, reading, and speaking. Reciprocal teaching can be easily integrated into standards-based instruction. This strategy is used to develop comprehension of expository text in which both the instructor and the students take turns leading a dialogue concerning sections of a text. This is a natural situation that occurs daily in the media center. In this strategy, students and instructors establish a dialogue and work together in comprehending text; thus, the result is deep analysis of the reading selection to improve comprehension.

RESEARCH FINDINGS

- Teachers who consistently use reciprocal teaching help their students develop better reading comprehension (Zarrillo, 2007).
- Reciprocal teaching and learning may be matched with learner needs and are particularly effective with students who have difficulties with traditional direct instructional methods (Grossman, 2004).
- This technique succeeds with small and large groups, in peer tutoring, in science instruction, and in teaching listening comprehension (Palincsar and Brown, 1986).
- This strategy is effective for generating personal interaction (Hashey and Connors, 2003).
- Reciprocal teaching has been found to be instrumental in increasing reading achievement of low-performing students in an urban school district as measured by standardized tests (Carter, 1997).
- This strategy can successfully be taught to low-achieving students, and once this strategy is learned, it increases reading achievement (Lysynchuk, Pressley, and Viye, 1990).
- The fact that students learn to develop their own questions about a given reading selection is advantageous in enhancing reading comprehension (Helfeldt and Henk, 1990).

STANDARDS

Information Literacy Standards: 2,3,4,5,6
NCTE/IRA Standards for the English Language Arts: 1,3,5,7,8, 10,11,12

STRATEGY NUTS AND BOLTS: IMPLEMENTATION IN THE LIBRARY OR CLASSROOM

The key to this strategy is to require students to think critically about the reading selection by constructing a list of questions from the reading passage. The students then ask the librarian or classroom teacher questions about what they read. The librarian or teacher, in turn, reinforces learning by answering the questions and, if necessary, helping students to refine their work into more focused questions.

This strategy enables students to read more decisively and analytically because they are reading to create and to answer questions. This comprehension strategy works nicely with content-specific texts such as science and social studies.

The following steps are used for the reciprocal teaching process:

1. Begin by introducing summarizing to students. Select a one- to two-paragraph selection and model how to write a summary statement with the entire group. When working in the library media center, the instructor can model summarizing for one student or a small group. This direct instruction is essential to teaching students how to summarize information effectively. Summarization is a skill often overlooked, so special attention should be paid to this skill.
2. Repeat this technique for each remaining piece of reciprocal teaching: questioning, clarifying, and predicting. It is important that these strategies be modeled appropriately for students. Each job can be described for students as the following:

   - Summarizer: Interact with group by discussing and documenting important parts of the selection.
   - Questioner: Ask questions related to the main ideas in the text, and be sure to include higher-level questions. Require members of the group to "read between the lines."
   - Clarifier: Help group members make connections between texts and their own background knowledge and previous experiences; help group members understand confusing parts of the text in addition to unknown vocabulary.
   - Predictor: Activate group members' background knowledge by making educated guesses and asking thought-provoking questions. In addition, help group members by making predictions, revising predictions, and/or confirming those predictions.

3. Divide the class into groups of four, and assign each group member a job title or allow students to choose their job

Name:

Predictor	Questioner	Clarifier	Summarizer

FIGURE 3.1: Reciprocal Teaching Organizer

according to their own interests or level of comfort. If working with an individual student, the librarian and student can alternate jobs.
4. Since significant modeling from the librarian or classroom teacher has occurred, students can begin to take responsibility for their jobs in groups using a selected passage. The librarian or classroom teacher helps students determine places in the text where they should stop and conduct their reciprocal teaching task. Students should be instructed to take turns providing the appropriate information to the group or librarian. Students can take on all four jobs simply by alternating roles at each predetermined stop. This method is recommended for students once they have practiced and used the strategy for some time and have become fluent in the implementation of the strategy. This can be accomplished over an extended period of time when students visit the library media center.
5. Distribute the Reciprocal Teaching Organizer in Figure 3.1 to students. As students read the text, they write the information in the appropriate column. During the reciprocal teaching, students can complete the graphic organizer with information learned from the group dialogue.
6. Begin the cycle again.

EXTENDING THE STRATEGY FOR DIVERSE LEARNERS AND STUDENTS WITH SPECIAL NEEDS

Because this strategy uses small segments of reading, it is an excellent one to implement for ELL students and students with special needs because it does not overwhelm them and thus promotes the improvement of reading comprehension for students who are adequate decoders. However, modifications of this procedure have been used to teach students who were poor decoders, second-language learners, or nonreaders. This strategy can be used with poor decoders as a read-along activity. Second-language learners can use it to practice developing skills, while nonreaders can learn by listening. Students who are good decoders can help other students in their group to interpret and understand what is being read. These stronger students with more experience in questioning can also stimulate deeper thinking and understanding in their less academically adept peers.

Another extension activity is to ask students who have read the passage to identify three or more sentences they'd like to discuss. Ask students to select sentences that support or challenge what they believe or sentences that confuse them. In a small group, have these students choose only one of the three sentences to offer the group. The first student reads a sentence aloud but doesn't make any comments. In turn, each of the remaining groups members reacts by agreeing, refuting, supporting, clarifying, commenting, or questioning. After everyone in the group has responded, the student who originally read the sentence summarizes.

COLLABORATIVE CONNECTIONS

Reciprocal teaching is ideally used with small groups of students, making it a perfect fit for the library media center; it creates a powerful synergy as students work toward a common academic goal. Generally, students can be grouped according to interest or assignment; the technique can then be implemented by the classroom teacher with support from the librarian. For example, as the teacher instructs students on how to summarize, the librarian can assist students in predicting, making connections, and/or clarifying—all basic steps in the research process.

Here is an example of a collaborative conversation that supports the reciprocal teaching concept. A ninth-grade science teacher collaborates with the librarian to find a reading selection on the Internet concerning the challenges facing rain forests.

Librarian/teacher: "A rainforest is an environment that receives high rainfall and is dominated by tall trees. A wide range of ecosystems fall into this category, of course, including the old-growth temperate forests of the Pacific Northwest. But most of the time when people talk about rainforests, they mean the tropical rainforests located near the equator. In the past hundred years, humans have begun destroying rainforests at an alarming rate. Today, roughly 1.5 acres of rainforest are destroyed every second. People are cutting down the rainforests in pursuit of three major resources: (1) Land for crops; (2) lumber for paper and other wood products; (3) land for livestock pastures." (reading passage available at <http://science.howstuffworks.com/rainforest1.htm>)

Librarian/teacher: (after reading the passage) "Who are some of the indigenous people of tropical rain forests? What is deforestation? What are some of the effects of deforestation on the rain forest?

What actions can environmentalists take to protect the rain forest?" Ask students to make a prediction about the rainforest. and create a graphic organizer to summarize and organize their information.

ASSESSMENT TOOLS

Listening to students during the dialogue is the most valuable means for determining whether or not they are reading comprehensively and moving beyond the factual level. The librarian or classroom teacher should take note of the types of questions being generated as a means of assessment. One should look for (1) questions about the meaning of particular words; (2) questions that are answered directly in the text; (3) questions that can be answered using common knowledge about the world; (4) questions that relate the text to students' own lives; (5) questions that ask "why"; and (6) questions that require student to locate information not contained in the text. The librarian or classroom teacher may check students' writing of questions. Students can monitor their own use of strategies by using the Self-Assessment of Reciprocal Teaching in Figure 3.2.

Where Can I Learn More about Reciprocal Teaching?

Palincsar, Annemarie. "The Quest for Meaning from Expository Text: A Teacher Guided Journey." In G. Duffy, L. Roehler, and J. Mason (Eds.), *Comprehensive Instruction.* New York: Longman, 1984, pp. 257–264.

Rosenshine, Barak, and Carla Meister. "Reciprocal teaching: A review of the research." *Review of Educational Research* (Winter 1994): 479–530.

Tierney, Robert J., and John E. Readence. *Reading Strategies and Practices: A Compendium.* 6th ed. Boston: Allyn & Bacon, 2005.

Web Extensions

<http://pers.dadeschools.net/prodev/model_lesson_.htm>
<http://forpd.ucf.edu/strategies/stratreciprocalteaching1.html>
<http://cst.cast.org/cst/guest/PAGE,resources-rt>
<http://www.readingquest.org/strat/rt.html>

Works Cited

Carter, Carolyn. "Why Reciprocal Teaching?" *Educational Leadership* (March 1997): 64–68.

Grossman, Herbert. *Classroom Behavior Management for Diverse and Inclusive Schools.* Landham, MD: Rowman & Littlefield, 2004.

Name: _____ Date:_____

Directions: Check the statements that are true.

Prediction Skills

_____ I predict before reading.

_____ I predict during reading.

_____ I revise and/or confirm my own predictions either orally or in my head.

Questioning Skills

_____ I ask the author(s) questions before reading.

_____ I ask the author(s) questions during reading.

_____ I ask questions about content before reading.

_____ I ask questions about content during reading.

_____ I strive to answer the questions I ask myself.

Clarification Skills

_____ When I don't understand a word, I use the context or surrounding words and/or sentences to figure out the meaning.

_____ I clarify or work to make sense of something that was confusing.

Summarization Skills

_____ I can recall important parts and/or details of what I have read.

_____ I can summarize or tell in my own words the important parts of the story.

FIGURE 3.2: Self-Assessment of Reciprocal Teaching

Harris, Tom. "How Rainforests Work." 17 April 2001. HowStuffWorks.com, http://science.howstuffworks.com/rainforest.htm.

Hashey, Jane M., and Diane. J. Connors. "Learn from Our Journey: Reciprocal Teaching Action Research." *The Reading Teacher* (November 2003): 224–232.

Helfeldt, John P., and William A. Henk. "Reciprocal Question-Answer Relationships: An Instructional Technique for At-Risk Readers." *Journal of Reading* (April 1990): 509–514.

Lysynchuk, Linda, et al. "Reciprocal Teaching Improves Standardized Reading Comprehension Performance of Poor Comprehenders." *Elementary School Journal* (May 1990): 469–484.

Palincsar, Annemarie Sullivan, and Ann L. Brown. "Interactive Teaching to Promote Independent Learning from Text." *The Reading Teacher* (April 1986): 771–777.

Palinscar, Annemarie, and Ann L. Brown. "Reciprocal Teaching of Comprehension-Fostering and Comprehension Monitoring Activities." *Cognition and Instruction* (March 1984): 117–175.

Zarrillo, James. *Are You Prepared to Teach Reading? A Practical Tool for Self-Assessment.* Upper Saddle River, NJ: Pearson, 2007.

4

Anticipation Guides

DEFINITION

Anticipation guides, also known as reaction guides or prediction guides, are active prereading strategies that challenge preconceptions, focus students' attention during reading, and activate and access prior knowledge. Designed to concurrently increase students' content knowledge and reading comprehension while activating prior knowledge, anticipation guides prepare readers for text by asking them to react to a series of essential questions and statements related to the content material before they read it. This strategy helps students set a purpose for reading and clarify their ideas, opinions, and misconceptions about a topic by completing a guide. Additionally, the guide enables students to focus their attention on the major points during their reading and provide a framework for discussing the text after their reading. Students tend to be more engaged and invested in supporting their viewpoint when using an anticipation guide. The purpose is twofold: (1) to make connections to prior knowledge and experiences before reading, and (2) to provide reinforcement of key concepts after reading as well as challenge students' prior knowledge.

This strategy, developed by Readence, Bean, and Baldwin (1981), is designed to activate prior knowledge and to provide students with a purpose for reading. Anticipation guides may be used for students at any level. They are generally most useful for expository texts but may also be used with narrative texts. The anticipation guide consists of a list of statements related to a text students will be reading. Some statements are true, some are false, and some provoke deep discussion, controversy, and even disagreement.

RESEARCH FINDINGS

- Anticipation guides are excellent tools for developing critical thinking and promoting cross-cultural understanding (Conley, 1985).
- Students learn more effectively when they already know something about a content area and when concepts in that area mean something to them and to their particular background or culture (Peshkin 1992; Protheroe and Barsdate, 1992).
- Effective statements used in anticipation guides convey a sense of the major ideas that the student will encounter; activate and draw upon the students' prior experience; and challenge students' beliefs (Duffelmeyer, 1994).
- Students with prior knowledge of particular topics remember more information than do students with little or no prior knowledge (Kujawa and Huske, 1995).

STANDARDS

Information Literacy Standards: 2,3,4,5,6
NCTE/IRA Standards for the English Language Arts: 1,3,5,7,8, 10,11,12

STRATEGY NUTS AND BOLTS: IMPLEMENTATION IN THE LIBRARY OR CLASSROOM

Anticipation guides are valuable for three reasons: (1) Students need to connect what they already know with new information and to realize that they do already know something that will help them comprehend; (2) Students exposed to anticipation guides tend to become interested and participate in lively discussion both before and after the learning activity, which motivates reading; and (3) Reading and writing instruction are easily integrated when anticipation guides are used.

To develop an anticipation guide, follow these steps:
1. Choose text related to the curriculum or research topic.
2. Identify several major concepts related to the reading assignment that students are expected to learn.

Directions: Respond to each statement before reading. Respond to each statement after reading.

Prereading		Statement	Postreading	
Agree	Disagree		Agree	Disagree

FIGURE 4.1: Anticipation Guide Template

3. Using the Anticipation Guide Template in Figure 4.1, develop a list of four to six clear statements that relate to the content being covered. These statements should challenge students' preconceptions and include some true and false. (Note: stay away from generalizations and abstract statements.) Write statements for which information can be identified in the text that supports or opposes each statement.
4. Students respond to each statement before reading and defend their beliefs and opinions in the left column under the heading "Prereading."
5. Openly discuss student responses and predictions as a class or in small groups prior to reading. Note any recurring themes in the discussion. Also, note any opposing or contradictory points of view. It is also important to clarify a purpose for reading so that students see the connection between the anticipation guide and the required reading.
6. Instruct students to read the assignment silently or orally depending on the audience and the purpose for reading. Instruct students to write comments on their answer sheets, noting agreement and disagreement between their answers and the author's message or purpose.
7. After reading, students respond to each statement in the right column under the heading "Postreading."
8. Students engage in a summarizing discussion, expressing how the reading selection reinforced or challenged their prior knowledge.

EXTENDING THE STRATEGY FOR DIVERSE LEARNERS AND STUDENTS WITH SPECIAL NEEDS

When working with ELL students, provide a list of the themes and require students to generate a list of statements for an anticipation guide. Have students chose one (or more) statements and "track them" throughout the piece of literature. Engage students in discussion to bring closure. Another technique is to do quick writes to a prompt such as: *Take five minutes to write about what friendship means to you. Use examples and brainstorm characteristics of a good friend.* Keeping a journal is another excellent strategy for diverse learners. A sample journal prompt might be: *How do you feel about voting? Give examples and support your opinion.* Another strategy is to permit "think time" and to use think-pair-share strategies to think about answers before having students respond. For students with special needs, pairing students together to read and respond to each statement is helpful.

COLLABORATIVE CONNECTIONS

Keeping in mind that effective practice recognizes that students' background knowledge influences learning outcomes, the librarian and the teacher can work together to prepare an anticipation guide based on a research topic, a selected reading, an event, a social issue, a time period, or a required book or novel to prime students' cognitive skills for what is to come. The reading can be from a traditional book, newspaper, or magazine or from an electronic text.

Another example of a collaborative connection is to have the librarian select a novel that complements the classroom teacher's lesson topic. The librarian can design an anticipation guide based on the book's themes that will help to structure students' initial thinking about the novel before students begin to read. The librarian can set up this anticipation guide as a threaded discussion. A wiki categorized by topic and subtopics will work quite nicely, as well.

ASSESSMENT TOOLS

Informal assessment is most likely the most appropriate for this activity. Through discussion and engagement with text, students come to understand what they do and do not understand about a given topic. It is imperative that the librarian or classroom teacher spend time discussing the preconceptions and misconceptions associated with any given topic. Before using an anticipation guide, it is essential that the librarian or classroom teacher have a clear purpose in mind for using the strategy. Students can easily see what they have learned from a text by comparing their "Prereading" and "Postreading" answers. Ask students to share their success, either in writing or orally. An example of an anticipation guide can be found in Figure 4.2, and the Anticipation Guide Self-Assessment in Figure 4.3 can be distributed to students as a technique for self-checking.

Anticipation Guide Example

Directions: In the column titled "Before Reading" write A for agree or D for disagree after reading each statement. Do the same in the "After Reading" column upon completion of reading and class discussion.

Before Reading A=Agree D=Disagree	Topic: Shakespeare	After Reading
	Romeo and Juliet is considered a tragedy because of the protagonists in the story.	
	Queen Mab is a well-known queen that Shakespeare introduced to literature in his first play, *Othello*.	
	The Cobbe portrait is considered to be the only authentic image of Shakespeare made during his lifetime.	
	Twelfth Night was first performed in 1604 at a law school in London.	
	As You Like It was the first comedy written by Shakespeare.	

FIGURE 4.2: Anticipation Guide Example

Use this page to help track your learning during the reading. Additionally, this will serve as your self-assessment for use of an Anticipation Guide.

Making Personal Connections

Question I have before reading	Page where I found the answer	How does this information fit into what I already know about the topic?	This reminds me of . . .	I wonder . . .	I don't understand . . .

FIGURE 4.3: Anticipation Guide Self-Assessment

Where Can I Learn More about Anticipation Guides?

Duffelmeyer, Fredrick A. "Effective Anticipation Guide Statements for Learning from Expository Prose." *Journal of Reading* (March 1994): 452–457.

Duffelmeyer, Fredrick A., et al. "Maximizing Reader-Text Confrontation with an Extended Anticipation Guide." *Journal of Reading* (November 1987): 146–150.

Head, M. H., and John. E. Readence. "Anticipation Guides: Meaning through Prediction." In E. K. Dishern, T. W. Bean, J. E. Readence, and D. W. Moore (Eds.), *Reading in the Content Areas*. 2nd ed. Dubuque, IA: Kendall/Hunt, 1986, pp. 229–234.

Herber, Harold. *Teaching Reading in Content Areas*. Englewood Cliffs, NJ: Prentice Hall, 1978.

Lenski, Susan D., et al. *Reading and Learning Strategies for Middle and High School Students*. Dubuque, IA: Kendall/Hunt, 1999.

Manzo, Anthony V., et al. *Content Area Literacy: Interactive Teaching for Active Learning*. New York: Wiley, 2001.

Merkley, Donna J. "Modified Anticipation Guide." *Reading Teacher* (Dec. 1966–Jan. 1997): 365–368.

Web Extensions

<http://reading.ecb.org/downloads/pk_lp_AnticipationGuide.pdf>
<http://www.lessonplanet.com/search?grade=All&keywords=anticipation+guide+science&rating=3&search_type=narrow>
<http://www.learnnc.org/reference/anticipation%20guide>
<http://www.indiana.edu/~l517/anticipation_guides.htm>
<http://www.ncrel.org/sdrs/areas/issues/students/learning/lr1anti.htm>

Works Cited

Conley, Mark. "Promoting Cross-Cultural Understanding through Content Area Reading Strategies." *Journal of Reading* (April 1985): 600–605.

Duffelmeyer, Fredrick A. "Effective Anticipation Guide Statements for Learning from Expository Prose." *Journal of Reading* (March 1994): 452–457.

Kujawa, Sandra, and Lynn Huske. *The Strategic Teaching and Reading Project Guidebook*. Rev. ed. Oak Brook, IL: North Central Regional Educational Laboratory, 1995.

Peshkin, Alan. "The Relationship between Culture and Curriculum: A Many Fitting Thing." In P. W. Jackson (Ed.), *Handbook on Research on Curriculum*. New York: Macmillan, 1992, pp. 248–267.

Protheroe, Nancy J., and Kelly J. Barsdate. "Culturally Sensitive Instruction." *Streamlined Seminar* 10, no. 4 (March 1992): 1–4.

Readence, John, et al. *Content Area Reading: An Integrated Approach*. Dubuque, IA: Kendall/Hunt, 1981.

5

Questioning the Author

DEFINITION

Questioning the Author (QtA) is a comprehension strategy that evokes interaction and engagement with text. When students read informational text, research shows that they construct very little meaning from the text because of obstacles such as incoherence, lack of clear descriptions and explanations, insufficient background knowledge, language barriers, and the assumption that the author is all-knowing and infallible (Reutzel and Cooter, 2009). Questioning the author gives readers the tools necessary to "grapple with text and depose the authority of the text" (McKeown, Beck, and Worthy, 1996, p. 561). Students learn that sometimes authors' ideas are not clearly written, moving the blame for the reader's lack of comprehension from the reader to the author. In other words, students are given the freedom to deal with text without the authority of the author watching over them as they read. Essentially, students are taught to "question" authors' intentions, purpose, and authority when reading. Reading is more than just extracting information; it is building understanding by determining what the information means (Beck, McKeown, Hamilton, and Kucan, 1997).

The Questioning the Author (QtA) strategy is based on the constructivist view of learning in which "learners need to actively use information, rather than simply collect pieces of information" (Beck et al., 1997, p. 8). QtA is geared to help students "consider meaning, to develop and grapple with ideas, and to try construct meaning"

(Beck et al., 1997, p. 6). Unique to QtA (Beck, McKeown, Hamilton, and Kucan, L., 1997; Beck, McKeown, Sandora, Kucan and Worthy, 1996) is the idea that textbook authors are not all knowing but are fallible and capable of unintentionally misinforming readers. By teaching students and teachers to question author's credibility, this strategy can potentially shift comprehension problems from the student to the author of the text. Ultimately, QtA (Beck et al., 1996) has four important features that aid students in comprehending the text: (1) It addresses text as the product of a fallible author; (2) it deals with text through general probes for meaning directed toward making sense of ideas in the text; (3) it takes place in the context of reading as it initially occurs; and (4) it encourages collaboration in the construction of meaning (p. 387).

RESEARCH FINDINGS

- Use of the QtA strategy changes dramatically the types of questions teachers asked. Teachers shifted from simply retrieving information to constructing meaning, "particularly in extending the construction of meaning" (Beck et al., 1996, p. 395).
- QtA improves teacher-to-student questions, student-to-student questions and classroom communication (Beck, McKeown, Sandora, Kucan, and Worthy, 1996).
- Reviews of research findings on questioning contend that it is an effective way "to stimulate student interaction, thinking and learning" (Wilen, Ishler, Hutchinson, and Kindsvatter, 2000).
- QtA provides opportunities for collaboration (Beck, McKeown, Hamilton, and Kucan, 1996).

STANDARDS

Information Literacy Standards: 2,3,4,5,6
NCTE/IRA Standards for the English Language Arts: 3,7,11,12

STRATEGY NUTS AND BOLTS: IMPLEMENTATION IN THE LIBRARY OR CLASSROOM

Questioning the Author (QtA) is an active reading pedagogical strategy that employs questions to increase student engagement with text at varying levels. Beck, McKeown, Sandora, Kucan, and Worthy (1996) developed Questioning the Author (QtA) technique to help students become actively involved in reading text *during* the reading process. This strategy differs significantly from other active engagement strategies that concentrate on interaction with text *after* it is read. QtA focuses on having "students grapple with and reflect on what an author is trying to say in order to build a representation from it" (p. 387). While students are reading, teachers pose *queries*, which are designed to support and encourage students as they deal with texts. The queries are designed to invite "understanding, interpretation, and elaboration by having students explore the meaning of what is written in the texts they read" (p. 387).

The Question the Author strategy has three main components: planning the implementation, creating queries, and developing discussions.

The following steps can be used as a guide to effectively use QtA:

1. Before using the strategy, prepare students by informing them that they will be learning a new way of reading and dealing with text. Be sure to advise students that learning a new way of reading text will take time, patience, and practice, so they should not expect immediate results.
2. The librarian or classroom teacher should make it clear to students that any author can be fallible. Letting students know that the content presented represents someone's ideas and that a person can sometimes makes mistakes will provide students the opportunity to understand that they have the right to question the author.
3. Model for students parts of QtA by first selecting a piece of text and then demonstrating the kinds of thoughts and considerations a reader should have when reading. Require students to follow along using a copy of the text either on an overhead projector or a document camera. If working in the library, the librarian or classroom teacher may want to give students their own individual copies. The teacher should read aloud, stop at difficult or interesting parts, and think aloud about anything that is confusing (Refer to Chapter 1, on think alouds). The librarian or classroom teacher should ensure that she is reading aloud sections where the author's writing is confusing or not clear. This is a perfect opportunity for students to share their own

experience with text. Ask students the following questions: What did you find confusing while reading? How would you write or communicate that part differently? What do you think the author is trying to say? What was written clearly and succinctly? This modeling of the think aloud and discussion is an important step and should be modeled several times if necessary. It is also important to inform students that they will be responsible for this type of interaction and engagement with text.

4. Planning for QtA involves three considerations (Beck et al., 1997): (1) Identifying the major understandings students should construct and anticipating potential problems in the text; (2) segmenting the text to focus on information needed to build understanding; and (3) developing queries that promote understanding. First, the librarian or classroom teacher critically reads the texts and identifies any major concepts that students must construct from the text while anticipating any problems that readers may encounter. The librarian or classroom teacher should consider this exercise a conversation with the author; a chance to get to the root of all understanding and problems with the text. "Teachers who find themselves doing extra work when they read can be reasonably sure that their students also will encounter difficulties and may not be able to resolve the problems without support" (Beck et al., 1997, p. 51).

5. Next, the librarian or classroom teacher must segment the text by determining where to stop reading in order to initiate the query that will develop into a discussion. It is important to note that the text should be segmented where understanding should occur or where confusion may occur. It is not necessary to stop at the end of paragraphs or sections.

6. The librarian or classroom teacher must then create and develop *queries*. Queries are a vital part of the QtA process and differ significantly from questions. Questions are usually used to assess students' comprehension of text, evaluate individual student responses, or prompt teacher-to-student interactions. They are used before or after reading. Queries, on the other hand, assist students in grappling with text ideas to construct meaning or facilitate group discussions and are

used during initial reading (Beck et al., 1997). Questions have traditionally been teacher-initiated, whereas queries serve as the focal point of the lesson or interaction with text. Queries allow the librarian or classroom teacher to be a facilitator of the discussion in the library or classroom. There are three types of queries to be used during the reading: initiating, follow-up, and narrative. *Initiating* queries include: What is the author trying to say? What is the author's message? What is the author talking about?

7. The second type of query, *follow-up*, helps students look at "what the text *means* rather than what the text *says*" (Beck et al., 1997, p. 37). Examples of follow-up prompts include: What does the author mean? Does the author explain this clearly? Does this make sense with knowing what the author told us previously? Why do you think the author tells us this now?

8. Finally, the third type of query is used specifically with *narrative* text. These queries differ significantly from the queries used with expository text, since the structure and the nature of text differ in a story. Queries used for narrative text may deal with story structure, characters, and/or plot development. Examples of such queries include: How do things look for this character now? How has the author let you know that something has changed? Does that change make sense given what we know about the character(s)?

9. The librarian or classroom teacher can use the Query Tally Sheet in Figure 5.1 to document the types of queries asked while interacting with a text. This will ensure that fewer queries that check for knowledge and information retrieval are used and that more queries relating to constructing message and extending discussion are used.

10. Development of discussion is an important element of QtA. It is the job of the students to construct meaning from the text. The librarian or classroom teacher should spend little time explaining text to students; instead, students should be grappling with text and dealing with the uncertainty themselves with guidance from the librarian or classroom teacher.

11. Finally, the librarian or classroom teacher should repeat the queries for each segment or section of text.

Retrieve Information	Construct Message	Extend Discussion	Check Knowledge

FIGURE 5.1: Query Tally Sheet

EXTENDING THE STRATEGY FOR DIVERSE LEARNERS AND STUDENTS WITH SPECIAL NEEDS

Questioning the Author (QtA) can be extremely helpful for second-language learners or learners with special needs because it gives the reader tools to deal with difficult or inconsiderate texts. Many students accept the author as the authority on the subject written, so, for many students, this is one obstacle to overcome. Additionally, engaging diverse learners and learners with special needs in the discussion provides opportunities for comprehension of and engagement and interaction with text. The librarian or classroom teacher can provide students with a copy of the queries prior to reading so that the students can anticipate when the text will be segmented and a query asked or initiated. In order for students to perform this strategy independently, it might be helpful to provide students with the QtA Bookmark in Figure 5.2, which provides sample queries for students. This bookmark can be cut and laminated for distribution. Allow students to add their own queries as they begin to master the strategy.

COLLABORATIVE CONNECTIONS

The librarian can play a vital role in the implementation of QtA, which is a new way of dealing with text and extrapolating information and understandings from text. For classroom teachers, the support of the librarian is necessary. When students are dealing with information in any form, in either print or electronic form, librarians can help students by showing them how to segment text and initiate their individual queries. By supporting students in their pursuit of information, the librarian can play a crucial role in helping students understand texts in new and better ways.

Additionally, the librarian can assist the classroom teacher by identifying text summaries from the assigned materials and asking students to evaluate the summaries. For example, the librarian can select relevant articles or passages from the assigned text and prepare a guided practice for students. The librarian designates the original text and then prepares two or three summaries for students to evaluate on the basis of what they know about Questioning the Author. This exercise helps students understand that authors are fallible and that not all text is written as perfectly as we would think or hope. The librarian or classroom teacher can use the Summary Evaluation

Initiating Queries

What is the author trying to say here?
What is the author's message?
What is the author talking about?

Follow-Up Queries

What does the author mean?
Does the author explain this clearly?
Does this make sense based on what the author has told us?
How does this connect to what the author told us here?
Why do you think the author tells us this now?

Narrative Queries (use with stories)

How do things look for this character now?
How has the author let you know that something has changed?
How has the author settled this for us?

FIGURE 5.2: QtA Bookmark

Worksheet in Figure 5.3 to use with text. An alternative exercise is to have students write the summary from the original text and then use the above criteria to evaluate their work. This summarization exercise is an outstanding method to help develop students' information literacy skills.

ASSESSMENT TOOLS

Although formal assessment of QtA will most likely not occur in a library or even a classroom, for that matter, it is important to ensure that students begin to take ownership of the newly learned strategy. It is equally important that students begin to use the strategy on their own without prompting from the librarian or classroom teacher. This will take time and patience. More important, it may be helpful to monitor the progress of both your own strategies and students' use of QtA.

Where Can I Learn More about Questioning the Author?

Almasi, Janice F., et al. "The Nature of Engaged Reading in Classroom Discussions of Literature." *Journal of Literacy Research* (March 1996): 107–146.

Beck, Isabel L., and Margaret G. McKeown. "Developing Questions That Promote Comprehension: The Story Map." *Language Art* (November–December 1981): 913–918.

Beck, Isabel L., and Margaret G. McKeown. "Inviting Students into the Pursuit of Meaning." *Educational Psychology Review* (September 2001): 225–241.

Beck, Isabel L., and Margaret G. McKeown. "Questioning the Author: Making Sense of Social Studies." *Educational Leadership* (November 2002): 44–47.

Florida Center for Reading Research. "Questioning the Author: An Approach for Enhancing Student Engagement," http://www.fcrr.org/FCRRReports/PDF/QuestioningAuthorFinal.pdf. December 2008.

Keene, Ellin O., and Susan Zimmerman. *Mosaic of Thought: Teaching Comprehension in a Readers' Workshop*. Portsmouth, NH: Heinemann, 1997.

McKeown, Margaret G., and Isabel L. Beck. "Getting the Discussion Started." *Educational Leadership* (November 1999): 25–28.

McKeown, Margaret G., and Isabel L.Beck "Taking Advantage of Read Alouds to Help Children Make Sense of Decontextualized Language." In A. van Kleeck, S. A. Stahl, and E. B. Bauer (Eds.)., *Storybook Reading*. Mahwah, NJ: Erlbaum, 2003, pp. 159–176.

Summary Evaluation Worksheet

Original Text:

Summary A:

Criteria	Yes/No	Why? Why not?
Does the summary convey the information accurately?		
Is the summary too narrow or too broad?		
Does it convey all the important elements?		
Does it convey too much?		
Would someone else using the summary gain all she or he needed to know to understand the subject?		
If sequence is important, are items in the right order?		
Did the author leave out his or her opinion and just report an undistorted essence of the original content?		
Did he or she paraphrase successfully?		

FIGURE 5.3: Summary Evaluation Worksheet

Summary B:

Criteria	Yes/No	Why? Why not?
Does the summary convey the information accurately?		
Is the summary too narrow or too broad?		
Does it convey all the important elements?		
Does it convey too much?		
Would someone else using the summary gain all s/he needed to know to understand the subject?		
If sequence is important, are items in the right order?		
Did the author leave out his or her opinion and just report an undistorted essence of the original content?		
Did he or she paraphrase successfully?		

FIGURE 5.3: (continued)

McKeown, Margaret G., et al. "Questioning the Author: Strategies for Reading Comprehension." Available at http://www.readingquest.org/strat/qta.html.

Web Extensions

<http://www.crayola.com/lesson-plans/detail/write-to-the-author-lesson-plan/>
<http://www2.scholastic.com/browse/article.jsp?id=3751182>
<http://www.buddyproject.org/lessons/info.asp?id=89>
<http://www.adlit.org/strategies/19796>
<http://www.readingquest.org/strat/qta.html>

Works Cited

Beck, Isabel L., et al. *Questioning the Author: An Approach for Enhancing Student Engagement with Text.* Newark, DE: International Reading Association, 1997.

Beck, Isabel L., et al. "Questioning the Author: A Yearlong Classroom Implementation to Engage Students with Text." *Elementary School Journal* (March 1996): 385–414.

Reutzel, D. Ray, and Robert B. Cooter. *The Essentials of Teaching Children to Read: The Teacher Makes the Difference.* 2nd ed. Upper Saddle River, NJ: Prentice Hall, 2009.

Wilen, William, et al. *Dynamics of Effective Teaching.* 4th ed. New York: Longman, 2000.

6

Survey, Question, Read, Recite, Review

DEFINITION

Survey, Question, Read, Recite, and Review (SQ3R) is an instructional strategy originally described by Robinson (1970) that is used with expository or nonfiction text. This active reading strategy teaches students how to effectively organize and synthesize information for easy retrieval when needed. SQ3R is not only an efficient reading strategy but also a useful study skill when preparing for an exam. It is a five-step approach, which includes surveying the chapter before reading, asking questions about text while reading, reading the text, reciting what you've read after reading, and reviewing information learned after reading the text. This strategy helps students improve their comprehension because it emphasizes metacognitive skills. It is best adapted to expository material in which text supports such as subject headings are used, as in textbooks, scholarly articles, and well-designed Web sites to reinforce reading for information and reading for a purpose.

RESEARCH FINDINGS

- The strategy is called the grandfather of study strategies (Lipson and Wixson, 2003).
- SQ3R lends itself to independent student use (Huber, 2004).
- Studies speak to the benefits and positive results of using this approach (Bhat, Rapport, and Griffin, 2000).

- It is important that teachers teach students how to apply the steps and provide opportunities for students to practice using the strategy correctly (Anderson and Armbruster, 1984).
- Questions are essential to the learning process because students must have information to act on—evidence developed through their own experiences that can be related to the ideas and skills being taught (Sunal and Haas, 2002).
- Reviews of research findings on questioning contend that it is an effective way "to stimulate student interaction, thinking and learning" (Wilen, Ishler, Hutchinson and Kindsvatter, 2000).
- When assessing students' understanding of what they have read, teachers have historically engaged in question asking (Dunkin, 1978; Raphael and Wonnacott, 1985), so it is of paramount importance that students learn to ask their own questions when reading.

STANDARDS

Information Literacy Standards: 2,3,4,5,6
NCTE/IRA Standards for the English Language Arts: 3,7,11,12

STRATEGY NUTS AND BOLTS: IMPLEMENTATION IN THE LIBRARY OR CLASSROOM

This strategy is designed to help students understand, organize, and remember the main points presented in a text, either print or electronic. This strategy works best when students are able to read fluently and are able to use context to understand vocabulary. With that said, ample practice reading and sufficient work on context clues should be consistently reinforced.

This following students' needs are targeted by using this strategy:

- Becoming a more independent, strategic reader
- Developing study skills
- Developing strategies for recalling and remembering content
- Understanding content text structure

The acronym SQ3R stands for the five steps in the procedure:

1. **Survey:** Students preview the material in order to get the general idea and overall organizational format of the text to be read by scanning text supports such as the titles, headings, graphs, charts, and pictures. This step helps students connect to their prior knowledge on the subject and to organize and categorize what they read. When students make connections to self, the world, and other texts, their comprehension improves.
2. **Question:** Students actively ask the five questions while they read: Who? What? When? Where? Why? This step helps students establish a purpose for reading by formulating questions based on the headings and subheadings in the text, article, or electronic text. Teacher or text questions may be used, but the reader needs to learn to formulate questions based on the text subheadings. Students should turn the headings into questions. This step is designed to arouse curiosity and increase comprehension.
3. **Read:** Students read the material in search of answers to the questions that were formulated in the previous step. They locate concepts and facts and record and reduce information in the margins or on sticky notes. This step promotes an active search for answers to specific questions by forcing concentration for better comprehension. It also improves memory and aids in lengthening attention span.
4. **Recite:** Students close their books and attempt to answer the questions from memory. They can also try to recall the main ideas and the author's organization. This step encourages students to use their own words and not simply to copy from the text. This step also helps to improve memory skills and ensures greater understanding.
5. **Review:** Students looks through the text again to recall, reflect, and take notes on the main ideas, key points, and answers to questions. This step helps students to clarify relationships and checks for short-term recall.

The SQ3R Chart in Figure 6.1 and the SQ3R Checklist in Figure 6.2 can be used in a variety of ways. For instance, both can be distributed to students to use as they implement the strategy. Furthermore, either Figure 6.1 or Figure 6.2 can be used as an assessment tool.

SQ3R Chart

1. Survey	Skim and scan the reading assignment.	Note headings. Note main idea and key points.
2. Question	Turn the headings into questions.	List the questions here:
3. Read	Read to find the answers.	Answer the questions here:
4. Recite	Say the answers aloud.	
5. Review	Write notes to answers the questions.	Write the notes here:

FIGURE 6.1: SQ3R Chart

SQ3R Checklist

Survey (No more than five minutes)
___ 1. Read the preface or introduction to the chapter and scan the table of contents to fix in mind the chapter outline.
___ 2. Scan the title, headings, and subheadings.
___ 3. Read the author's summary.
___ 4. Read the introductory and concluding paragraphs.
___ 5. Study pictures, graphs, charts, etc. (visual summary of ideas presented).
___ 6. Concentrate on topic sentences and repeated words or phrases.
___ 7. Note italicized printing throughout chapter (underline for later reference).

Complete the question, read and recite for each section before moving to the next section.

Question
___ Formulate questions about the chapter content based on your preview reading. Who? What? When? Where? How? Why?

___ 1. Consider the following for possible questions:
    ___ a. Headings   ___ d. Author's summary
    ___ b. Subheadings   ___ e. Chapter introduction
    ___ c. Titles
___ 2. Jot down questions for later review.

Read
___ 1. Scan for answers to questions you posed.
___ 2. Summarize and restate ideas as you read.
___ 3. Make use of details as you learn the overall organization of the chapter (e.g., noting the relationship of paragraph to paragraph, key sentences to key sentences).
___ 4. Write down ideas in an attempt to remember key phrases or words.

FIGURE 6.2: SQ3R Checklist

Recite
___ 1. Test yourself now by verbalizing the answers to the questions you made up (check for immediate recall at the end of the first section, second section, etc.
___ 2. Use supporting materials to make general ideas clearer.
  ___ a. Comparisons
  ___ b. Contrasts
  ___ c. Statistics (e.g., 75% of the students)
  ___ d. Quotations from authorities
  ___ e. Vivid descriptions

Review (No more than ten minutes)
___ 1. Read:
  ___ the underlining (mode when marking the text)
  ___ the marginal notes
  ___ the summaries
___ 2. Section by section, look away from the book and recite the main points in each section. (If you cannot, reread the summaries.)

FIGURE 6.2: (continued)

EXTENDING THE STRATEGY FOR DIVERSE LEARNERS AND STUDENTS WITH SPECIAL NEEDS

Students with special needs and diverse learners may struggle with comprehension of text on their grade level, especially expository text. Sufficient support is necessary to help students monitor their comprehension and implement this complex, yet effective, strategy. Working cooperatively with several other students enhances students' abilities to talk through the material to be read and enables them to accept other viewpoints and ideas that they might have overlooked or misunderstood if they were working independently. Additionally, students can summarize the text using the Herringbone/Fishbone Graphic Organizer in Figure 6.3. Use of this graphic organizer can help visual learners organize information for better comprehension.

COLLABORATIVE CONNECTIONS

The librarian should consult with the classroom teacher regarding the topic of study and then recommend book chapters, articles, or Web sites that lend themselves to the unit of study. After the teacher selects the text, the teacher and the librarian work together to develop specific research tasks to complete the project. While conducting research and reading texts, students then use the SQ3R strategy. The librarian can support students as they conduct each step in the research process. Figures 6.1 and 6.2 can be posted in the library and/or distributed for student use during the research process. It is imperative that students be provided with consistent exposure to the SQ3R steps so that they can eventually complete the process automatically. Additionally, this strategy is a must when preparing students for research projects because it emphasizes two critical information literacy skills: formulating essential questions and paraphrasing. Students need help in the form of scaffolding; this strategy provides a framework for developing a schema for organizing information. It explicitly "walks" students through the complicated task of reading and transforming raw information. Teachers and librarians can confer with students to help them select the most promising questions to research. SQ3R charts can be generated at <http://www.tech-nology.com/web_tools/graphic_org/sq3r/search.>

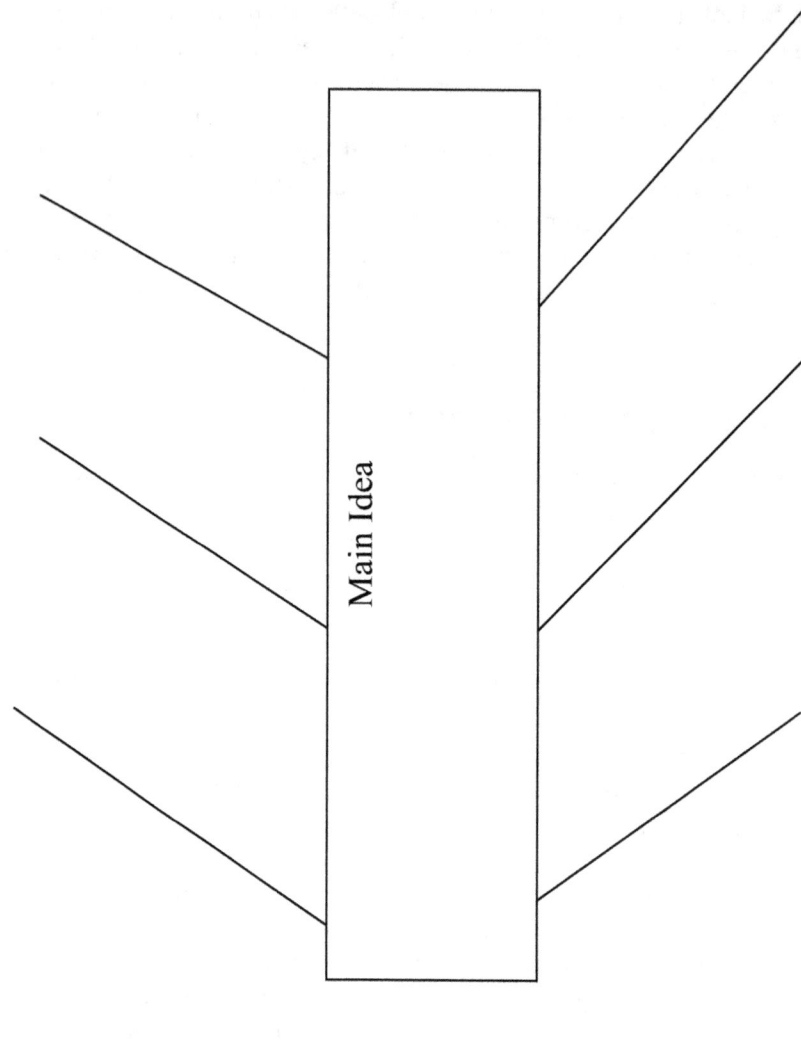

FIGURE 6.3: Herringbone/Fishbone Graphic Organizer

S__
E__
L__

ASSESSMENT TOOLS

Assessment can be completed orally with a peer, through rewriting notes from memory, or by comparing information to a master set of notes prepared by the librarian or classroom teacher. A mock quiz developed by a peer or the teacher can also be used to evaluate learning. An alternative is to assign students to write a one- to two-paragraph summary of the text using their notes from the SQ3R Checklist (Figure 6.2) or the prompt "What new things did you learn?"

Additionally, the T-chart in Figure 6.4 or the T-List in Figure 6.5 can be used to monitor students' progress through this five-step strategy.

Where Can I Learn More about SQ3R?

Irwin, Judith W., and Isabel Baker. *Promoting Active Reading Comprehension Strategies.* Englewood, NJ: Prentice Hall, 1989.

Paris, Scott G., et al. "Becoming a Strategic Reader." *Contemporary Educational Psychology* (August 1983): 293–316.

Powers, Michelle. "SQR3 Study Method." *Associated Content,* http://www.associatedcontent.com/article/316504/sqr3_study_method.html?page=2&cat=4. Rhoades, Lynn K., and Curt Dudley-Marling. *Readers and Writers with a Difference.* Portsmouth, NH: Heinemann, 1996.

Vacca, Richard, and Joanne Vacca. *Content Area Reading.* 3rd ed. Boston: Scott, Foresman, 1989.

Web Extensions

<http://gustaf.blc.edu/~education/auecker07/downloads/SQ3R%20Lesson%20plan.pdf>
<http://www.lpb.org/education/classroom/itv/litlearn/lessons/lssn_sq3r.pdf>
<http://www.teach-nology.com/worksheets/graphic/sq3r/>
<http://www.teach-nology.com/web_tools/graphic_org/sq3r/search.>

Works Cited

Anderson, Thomas H., and Bonnie B. Armbruster. "Studying." In P. D. Pearson, R. Barr, M. L. Kamil, and P. Mosenthal (Eds.), *Handbook of Reading Research.* New York: Longman, 1984, pp. 657–679.

Bhat, Preetha, et al. "A Legal Perspective on the Use of Specific Learning Methods for Students with Learning Disabilities." *Learning Disabilities Quarterly* (Fall 2000): 283–297.

Dunkin, Michael. "Student Characteristics, Classroom Practices, and Student Achievement." *Journal of Educational Psychology* (December 1978): 998–1009.

T-Chart

Main Ideas	Details or Examples

FIGURE 6.4: T-Chart

T-List

Reduce (Summarize in short phrases or essential questions next to each block of notes)	**Record** (Write notes on this side)

Review
Summarize in paragraph style your points or responses to the questions in three to five sentences. Reflect and comment on what you have learned.

FIGURE 6.5: T-List

Huber, Jennifer A. "A Closer Look at SQ3R." *Reading Improvement* (June 2004): 108–113.

Lipson, Marjorie Y., and Karen K. Wixson. *Assessment and Instruction of Reading and Writing Disability: An Interactive. Approach.* 3rd ed. New York: Allyn & Bacon, 2003.

Raphael, Taffy E., and C. A. Wonnacott. *Increasing Students' Sensitivity to Sources of Information: An Instructional Study in Question-Answer Relationships.* Cambridge, MA: Bolt, Beranek, & Newman, 1983.

Robinson, Frances. *Effective Study.* 4th ed. New York: Harper & Row, 1970.

Sunal, Cynthia S., and Mary E. Haas. *Social Studies for the Elementary and Middle Grades: A Constructivist Approach.* Boston: Allyn & Bacon, 2002.

Wilen, William, et al. *Dynamics of Effective Teaching.* 4th ed. New York: Longman, 2000.

PART II

Vocabulary Strategies for the Library and Classroom

7

Semantic Feature Analysis

DEFINITION

Semantic Feature Analysis is an instructional vocabulary strategy that assists students in developing and examining vocabulary by recognizing relationships and distinctions among words and concepts that can significantly improve comprehension. This strategy, which uses a chart or a grid to illustrate vocabulary words or concepts and the relationships between the words and concepts, can be used as a brainstorming activity at the beginning of a unit to activate students' prior knowledge or as a summarization activity to integrate and intertwine prior knowledge and new information. Semantic feature analysis can be used in all content areas to compare and contrast objects, people, ideas, and/or events. A semantic feature analysis grid allows for a visual representation of connections between and among words or concepts. Additionally, the grid helps students recognize what information they do not know, which can potentially lead to future research on that particular topic. Finally, a semantic feature analysis grid is an excellent means to generate class and small group discussion.

RESEARCH FINDINGS

- Semantic feature analysis is a means of displaying the relationship of the whole to the parts and the parts to the whole and allows information to be organized according to the connections that the reader sees so that even items separated in the

Chapter 7: Semantic Feature Analysis **69**

text can be placed near each other and connected (Sinatra, Stahl-Gemake, and Morgan, 1986).
- Semantic analysis forces students to think; this separates it from outlining, which is linear (Miccinati, 1988).
- Graphic overviews and displays help organize students' thoughts (Lambiotte and Dansereau, 1992; Rakes, Rakes, and Smith, 1995).
- When readers understand the relationships among concepts in a selection, they can begin to connect the new relationships to their previous knowledge (Richardson, Morgan, and Fleenner, 2006).
- Semantic maps are graphic representations that illustrate concepts and the relationships between concepts (Pearson and Johnson, 1978).
- If a student has no prior knowledge about a particular topic being discussed, then the student may not be able to understand the topic (Stein, Leinhardt, and Bickel, 1989).

STANDARDS

Information Literacy Standards: 2, 3,4,5
NCTE/IRA Standards for the English Language Arts Standards: 1,3,4,7,8,11,12

STRATEGY NUTS AND BOLTS: IMPLEMENTATION IN THE LIBRARY OR CLASSROOM

Semantic feature analysis is based on schema theory, which suggests that we learn by relating new information to the information we already know. Semantic feature analysis requires students to discover and identify more complex relationships and encourages students to make connections among concepts, story ideas, characters, and other information from a text selection. The analysis enables students to understand relationships and connections among topics and details as they read new material and retrieve new information. They have to analyze, evaluate, reason critically, organize, categorize, and show relationships and connections. Semantic feature analysis also allows students to easily "see" what they don't know, which can be invaluable to future learning.

Semantic mapping complements inquiry learning because it enables students to integrate information from multiple sources.

Semantic Feature Analysis Template

Name _____

FIGURE 7.1: Semantic Feature Analysis Template

Types of Government

	Dependence	Independence	Autonomy
Democracy			
Dictatorship			
Monarchy			
Oligarchy			
Theocracy			
Republic			

FIGURE 7.2: Semantic Feature Analysis Example

Semantic mapping requires students to make decisions about what information is important and to organize the information in some way. The following steps are used in the process:

1. Decide on elements (vocabulary words/concepts) to be compared and contrasted in the semantic feature analysis.
2. Using the Semantic Feature Analysis Template in Figure 7.1, create a grid containing the desired elements.
3. List the elements of the vocabulary words or concepts vertically on the left side of the grid.
4. List the criteria/features/categories across the top of the grid. See the Semantic Feature Analysis Example in Figure 7.2.
5. Students complete the grid by matching the word with the concepts. If the concept is associated with the feature or characteristic, the student records a Y or a + (plus sign) in the grid where that column and row intersect; if the feature is not associated with the concept, an N or – (minus sign) is placed in the corresponding square on the grid.
6. Students can then be asked to compare their responses in small groups or with partners and to share them with the whole class.

EXTENDING THE STRATEGY FOR DIVERSE LEARNERS AND STUDENTS WITH SPECIAL NEEDS

This strategy is particularly effective in extending vocabulary and thinking for ELL students whose cultural background and language may differ from those associated with the text. The semantic feature analysis strategy helps students organize newly learned information and synthesize that information with what they may already know about a subject while learning the new information they have just encountered. The librarian or classroom teacher can write each term on a note card and then have the students divide the cards into two piles: familiar terms and unfamiliar terms. Next, the students can create a concept map with the familiar terms and can guess the meanings of the unfamiliar terms. (This is far better than just telling them the meanings based on word parts, such as prefixes, suffixes, and root words. By guessing, students must become actively involved.) The librarian or classroom teacher can present increasingly rich context clues from the text's passage while discussing and refining the students' word guesses. The instructor can then direct students to look

Information Retrieval Analysis Chart

Topic of Study: _____

Information Sources	Essential Question	Essential Question	Essential Question	Essential Question

FIGURE 7.3: Information Retrieval Analysis Chart

up the meaning of the word in a print or online dictionary. Students should then be able to associate the unfamiliar words with the familiar words. Be sure students integrate their new words into the grid so that they can see the similarities and differences between words.

COLLABORATIVE CONNECTIONS

The librarian can partner with the classroom teacher to integrate information skills instruction to support the curricular content by creating a template for a unit of study.

For example, they can partner to create and use this semantic analysis as a prereading activity to analyze the attributes of a character or themes in a novel in a literature course or an historical figure from an American history course. The teacher and the librarian can determine the list of attributes and then identify distinct and nondistinct features for each concept, character, or theme. Additionally, because the semantic feature analysis is great for helping students develop patterns of understanding, this analysis strategy provides an easy way to help students narrow the focus of their research and quickly identify where they need more information. To begin the research process in the library, the librarian can prepare a chart like the Information Retrieval Analysis Chart in Figure 7.3 to help students take notes and monitor their progress while conducting research in the library. This chart can help the students identify information gaps and recognize the need to gather more information, a critical component in the information literacy process. Moreover, the librarian can use the semantic feature analysis strategy to teach students to analyze different types of reference sources, such as primary sources, that they could use during the research process.

ASSESSMENT TOOLS

Keep in mind that the students' semantic feature analysis grids will vary with the prior level of knowledge of each student. Small-group sharing of the semantic maps allows students to compare and to evaluate their own choices in terms of information and organization. Although formal assessment of a semantic feature analysis grid is not recommended, informal assessment is vital for classroom teachers and librarians. Through observation and classroom discussion, librarians and classroom teachers can easily determine what students do and do not know about a given topic. This knowledge gives librarians and classroom teachers the power to meet students where they are and to guide them through the process of learning more about a topic.

Where Can I Learn More about Semantic Feature Analysis?

Crawley, Sharon J. "Using Semantic Mapping to Help Students Organize Social Studies Text." *Journal of the Middle States Council for the Social Studies* 10 (Fall 1988): 24–29.

Gifford, Ann Porter. "Broadening Concepts through Vocabulary Development." *Reading Improvement* 37, no. 1 (Spring 2000): 2–12.

Maddux, Clebourne D., et al. *Educational Computing: Learning with Tomorrow's Technologies.* 3rd ed. Boston: Allyn & Bacon, 2001.

Watts, S., and Truscott, D. M. "Using Contextual Analysis to Help Students Become Independent Word Learners." *The NERA Journal* 32, no. 3 (1996): 13–20.

Web Extensions

<http://www.readwritethink.org/lessons/lesson_view.asp?id=240>
<http://teacher.neisd.net/lesson_plans/master_results.cfm?recordID=B3A7211A-508B-FD7A-2C9199FDCB0358D1>
<http://www.buddyproject.org/lessons/info.asp?id=45>
<http://www.enchantedlearning.com/graphicorganizers/sfa/>
<http://www.readingquest.org/strat/sfa.html>
<http://www.columbia.k12.mo.us/she/cncptmap.html>

Works Cited

Lambiotte, Judith G., and Donald. F. Dansereau. "Effects of Knowledge Maps and Prior Knowledge on Recall of Science Lecture Content." *Journal of Experimental Education* 60, no. 3 (Spring 1992): 189–201.

Miccinati, Jennette L. "Mapping the Terrain: Connecting Reading with Academic Writing." *Journal of Reading* 31, no. 6 (March 1988): 542–552.

Pearson, P. David, and David Johnson. *Teaching Reading Comprehension.* New York: Holt, Rinehart, & Winston, 1978.

Rakes, Glenda C., et al. "Using Visuals to Enhance Secondary Students' Reading Comprehension of Expository Texts." *Journal of Adolescent & Adult Literacy* 39, no. 1 (September 1995): 46–54.

Richardson, Judy S., et al. *Reading to Learn in the Content Areas.* Belmont, CA: Thompson/Wadsworth, 2006.

Sinatra, Richard, et al. "Using Semantic Mapping after Reading to Organize and Write Original Discourse." *Journal of Reading* 30, no. 1 (October 1986): 4–13.

Stein, Mary, et al. "Instructional Issues for Teaching Students at Risk." In R. E. Slavin, N. L. Karweit, and N. A. Madden (Eds.), *Effective Programs for Students at Risk.* Boston, MA: Allyn & Bacon, 1989, pp. 145–195.

8

Word Questioning Maps/Word Journals

DEFINITION

A word questioning map is a vocabulary strategy that utilizes a graphic organizer to help students make associations of meanings for new terms and conquer challenging vocabulary. This vocabulary-building strategy encourages students to investigate the origins and meaning of words, terms, phrases, word families, and concepts related to the text, class discussions, or daily routines. The intent of this strategy is to build interest in vocabulary while encouraging the student to collect and examine terms.

The word journal provides an efficient means of collecting and recording predetermined or self-selected words, terms, and concepts and of exploring and assimilating new vocabulary words into students' existing vocabulary. In order for new vocabulary to become part of a student's working lexicon, the student must attach meaning to the word and categorize the word within his or her mental framework while experiencing multiple exposures to the word. This strategy can be readily used in conjunction with other learning strategies to develop literacy skills, note-taking skills, and other information literacy and reference skills.

RESEARCH FINDINGS

- Vocabulary plays a critical role in reading by facilitating comprehension (Blachowitz and Fisher, 2000; Pressley, 2002; Snow, Burns, and Griffin, 1998).

- Vocabulary instruction is one of the five key emphasis areas necessary for successful reading among students (National Reading Panel, 2000).
- There is a strong link between vocabulary and reading comprehension (Anderson and Nagy, 1991; Baker et al., 1998; Blachowitz and Fisher, 2000; National Reading Panel, 2000).
- Extensive reading of many kinds of material both in school and outside results in substantial growth in vocabulary and comprehension abilities and in the information base of students (Cawelty, 2004).
- Students acquire many new words from reading widely, listening to stories, and talking about words (Nagy, 1988; Smith and Elley, 1994).
- The more vocabulary words students know, the better able they are to infer unfamiliar words (Rupley et al., 1998–1999).
- Listening to challenging material that builds a student's background knowledge may well be the most effective way to increase vocabulary (Carver and Leibert, 1995).
- A brief explanation of new words—in the context of the story—seems to help students remember new vocabulary (Brett et al., 1996).

Librarians and classroom teachers should consider one important pedagogical technique: Less is more. That is, depth is more when it comes to teaching new vocabulary terminology. It is very important to teach fewer vocabulary terms but to teach them in a manner that results in deep understandings of each term. Also, librarians and classroom teachers should consider teaching terms that will be used repeatedly throughout the semester to ensure that students receive multiple exposures to the same word(s) in multiple contexts. These are foundational concepts upon which a great deal of information will be built over the long term. Finally, librarians and classroom teachers must teach terms that are central to the unit or theme of study and terms that are so important that if students do not understand them, they are likely to have difficulty understanding the remainder of the unit (Ellis, 2002).

STANDARDS

Information Literacy Standards: 1,2,3,6
NCTE/IRA Standards for the English Language Arts: 1,2,4,5,6, 8,9,11,12

STRATEGY NUTS AND BOLTS: IMPLEMENTATION IN THE LIBRARY OR CLASSROOM

The focus of effective vocabulary instruction is to help students expand their knowledge of word meanings, thus resulting in an expanded reading, writing, listening and speaking vocabulary. As students strive to become proficient readers, they will encounter vocabulary in their reading material and concepts that they have not run across in previous reading or that do not know or use in their speaking or writing vocabulary. Knowing a word involves more than identification and pronunciation. It involves understanding the word in a conversation, using the word in speech and writing, and understanding the word in the context of print. These basic vocabulary strategies are key presearch activities that are essential to search success and in creating an information-seeking strategy that, according to research, has been a problem for student researchers. Successful searches rely on students' abilities to interchange terms and to use them appropriately when conducting independent research.

In accordance with the research findings mentioned earlier, librarians and teachers should plan five categories of activities to expand students' reading vocabularies. These categories are:

1. Increasing the amount of time students read independently
2. Increasing the different types of texts that students encounter
3. Teaching students the meanings of key words related to curricular content
4. Teaching strategies for contextual analysis so that students can figure out the meanings of words they do not know
5. Encouraging word consciousness

Students must be able to connect the word to what they already know. While teaching the new term in context of a subject-matter lesson is a critical instructional technique, an equally important elaboration technique is for students to relate the term to something with which the students are already familiar. There is a wide array of methods by which students can formulate knowledge connections. For example, they can identify how the term is related to previous subject-matter they have learned; they can identify something from their personal life experiences that the term reminds them of; they can create metaphors or similes for the term; or they can say how the term relates to understanding or solving some real-life problem. An essential part of this elaboration process is having the students explain the connection. For example, the students should say not only what personal experience the word makes them think of but also why it reminds them of that word.

Word Questioning Map

The following are two approaches to using a word questioning map. The first is used in a whole-class setting and is teacher-directed. This approach may be most appropriate for diverse learners and students with special needs. The second approach is a student-centered approach.

Using the first approach, the librarian or classroom teacher can begin discussing new vocabulary by asking the following questions in a whole-class setting.

1. What parts of the words do you recognize?
2. Have you ever heard the word?
3. Do you have any idea what it means?
4. What if I tell you the word is related to (provide example)?
5. Which word was difficult for you?
6. Listen to this sentence. Now can you use the word in a sentence? Can you figure out the meaning from the context?

The second approach outlines the steps to constructing a word questioning map using the Word Questioning Map in Figure 8.1.

1. The classroom teacher and the librarian prepare a vocabulary list on the selected topic. For example, if students are studying ecosystems, some of the terms might include *biotic, abiotic, biomes, flora, fauna, climate, environment, precipitation, temperature, elevation, terrain, adaptation, soil,* and *ecologist.*
2. Students can work individually, with a partner, or in groups to construct the Word Questioning Map in Figure 8.1.
3. The classroom teacher or librarian assigns a target word to each student or group.
4. Students complete the word questioning map in Figure 8.1 and share their findings with the class.
5. As an extension activity, students can create a Venn diagram to illustrate the relationships between and among the target words.

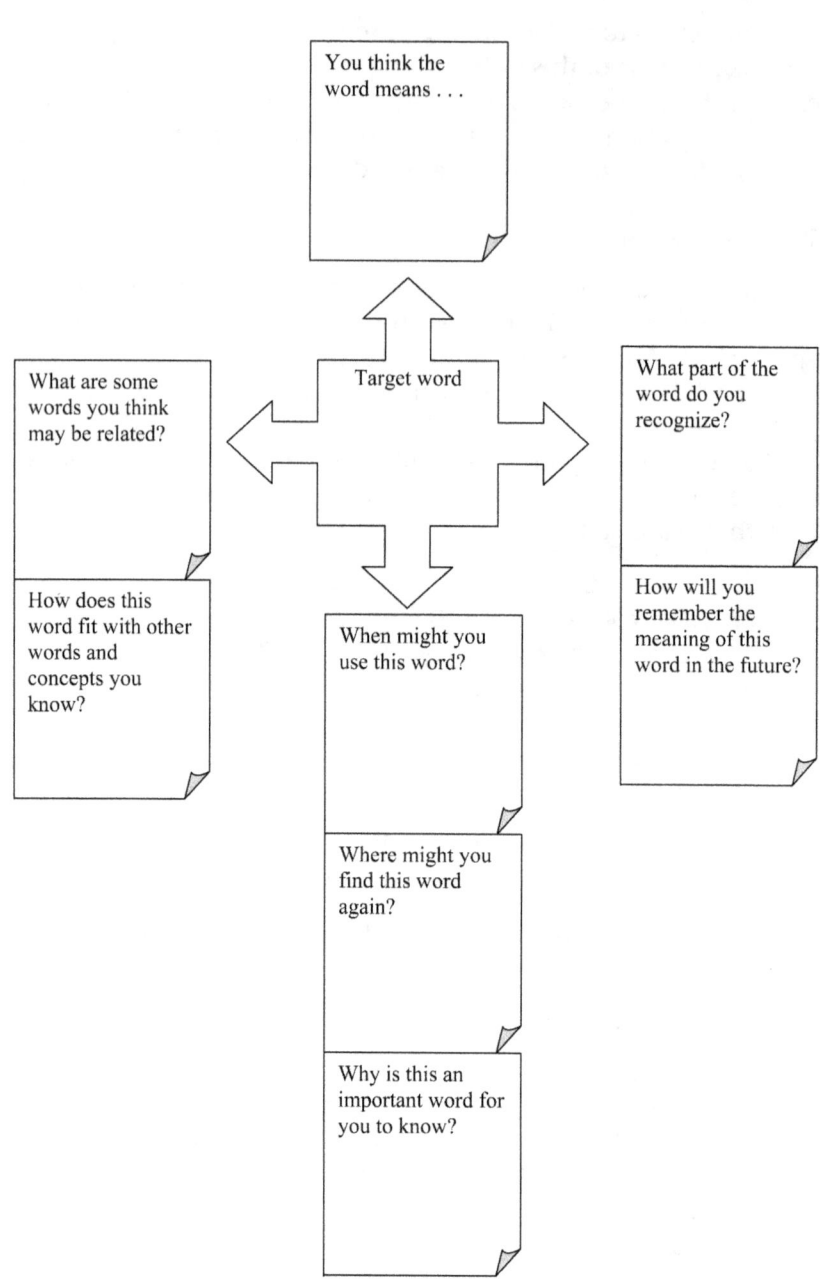

FIGURE 8.1: Word Questioning Map

In sum, word questioning maps can become very complex and require a great deal of your time and attention, but they are useful in organizing, learning, and demonstrating what students know about a particular topic and helping them to make connections and relationships between and among the various new vocabulary terms.

Word Journals

Word journals enable students to attach meaning to a word as well as to categorize it. Students rank the words or categorize them as most important or least important. This activity helps students begin to see that all words in the text are not equally important and that information needs to be categorized. The teacher or librarian can have students organize the words into a diagram using software like Inspiration© or Kidspiration© if available. Students can use the Rapid Fire tool to create graphic organizers with visual elements and vocabulary connections.

The librarian or classroom teacher introduces a new vocabulary term, and, in their journals, the students write the term and the sentence where it is found and note whether they are acquainted with the word. Then students can work in groups to define the word and write sentences, telling how the word is used in the article or story. As the story progresses and students become familiar with the technique, they can offer words and define and use them in this manner. A variation of this method is to create a hyperlinked word journal whose purpose is to expand vocabulary and to promote reading fluency. Students can work individually or in groups to create these hyperlinked journals. Ask students to compose their own story using the prescribed sets of vocabulary words selected by the librarian and the teacher. Students create a hyperlink to the vocabulary words. Indicate to students that the hyperlinks can be connected to PowerPoint® slides they create to illustrate the meaning of the each word or to Web sites they have located on the Internet. Visit <http://www.technologyintegrationforteachers.com> to view links to sample stories that illustrate the use of hyperlinks and provide additional suggestions for the use of hyperlinked journals.

The librarian can create a blog that students can use as a cyberjournal where they are required to write their thoughts about their daily activities or any assigned topic using targeted words. Some useful blog sites where librarians/teachers can find some good ideas are <http://wwwesigo.net> and <http://blog-ef;/blogspot.com>.

The librarian can create a chat room or a discussion group on the school server. These are two excellent tools that help students to learn from one another, to "talk" to one another, and to attempt to use their new vocabulary terms in the process.

Additionally, teachers and librarians can pose questions about key terms and phrases for students to consider in their journals to stimulate student thinking. These student word journals can become a permanent artifact of the research process and a personal resource that can be used as a springboard to the next project and as a tutorial for review before the next project begins.

Yet another technique is to have students choose at least three important words each week that they want to know the meaning of. The words can come from any book or article or Web site related to the content being studied. Students should include the date, the title, and the author, the page number, the word, how it is used, and what the student thinks the words mean. The students can then use the dictionary (either in print or online) to check for accuracy.

Here's an example:

Date: January 12, 2009
Title: The Lion, the Witch, and the Wardrobe
Author: C. S. Lewis
Page: 40
Word: probable
How used: "nothing is more probable . . ."
Your meaning: Likely, very possible
Dictionary meaning:

EXTENDING THE STRATEGY FOR DIVERSE LEARNERS AND STUDENTS WITH SPECIAL NEEDS

One of the best methods to assist diverse learners is to have them create mnemonic pictures or stories that capture the essence of a new term's meaning. For example, have students create wordless PowerPoint® slides that incorporate the new vocabulary to invent stories. Another method is to have students pick a theme and create an alphabet book using digital photos to illustrate the meaning of the words. These alphabet books can then be shared with elementary students.

Another strategy that can assist ELL and special-needs students is to have students define a word on a piece of drawing paper, then find a picture or make an original drawing that illustrates the concept. Below the picture, students use the term in a sentence that clarifies or goes along with what is happening in the picture or drawing. This exercise can also be done in the students' word journals.

Students whose first language is not English may struggle with abstract terms. By relating the abstract to something concrete and to a visual support, librarians and classroom teachers can help students retain the new word or concept. It may also be beneficial to help these students keep an ongoing dictionary of terms learned throughout a unit of study or over the course of a semester or school year. Finally, word walls can be helpful in helping diverse learners and can provide the visual stimulus that some students need.

COLLABORATIVE CONNECTIONS

The librarian and the classroom teacher can work together to create words lists, usually 10 words in each list for every reading level. They can select an article and create a word hunt for students that is based on the important terms that they suspect will be new to students. Additionally, the librarian and the classroom teacher can make a vocabulary chart to go along with the book or articles or one that is associated with the primary unit of study.

The librarian or the classroom teacher can collaboratively select 10 to 15 words from the content that students need to know and place the words randomly on a page, transparency, or PowerPoint® slide. Students work in groups of two (partner A and partner B). Each selects a word and writes it on a slip of paper so that the partner cannot see it. Partner A asks questions of partner B that can be answered with "yes" or "no" to determine the secret word. As they ask questions, the students keep a tally. The student who figures out the secret word using the fewest questions is the winner. The value in this activity is the close examination of words as students consider what kinds of questions will narrow the field.

To incorporate the use of technology into the teaching of vocabulary, the librarian and the classroom teacher may select a target word from the article and have student contribute words they associate with it and type the words using the Rapid Fire tool on Inspiration©. The words are immediately added to a web with connecting lines, providing a visual. If Inspiration© is not available, this exercise can be done by dividing students into groups of two or three. Appoint a student to be the recorder. Have the students each contribute a word they associate with the target word while the recorder creates the word questioning map by hand on construction or butcher paper.

ASSESSMENT TOOLS

Matching tests can be used to assess students' knowledge of key terms and concepts. It is recommended that there be more response choice items (possible answers) than stimulus items (words or phrases to be matched) to help compensate for guessing. A completion test can also be designed.

Students should use the new term themselves in a sentence within the context of a discussion of broader topics. As students collect intriguing words, have them share them once every week or two. Students can generate and display a class list, use the dictionary to define unfamiliar words, or engage in word play with root words, prefixes, and suffixes. Select two or three words for the class to use on a regular basis.

The use of journals, monitored by the teacher or librarian, to chronicle student experience and track progress is also an effective assessment technique.

Where Can I Learn More about Word Questioning Maps/Word Journals?

Bear, Donald R., and Shane Templeton. "Explorations in Developmental Spelling: Foundations for Learning and Teaching Phonics, Spelling, and Vocabulary." *The Reading Teacher.* (November 1998): 222–242.

Bear, Donald R., et al. *Words Their Way: Word Study for Phonics, Vocabulary, and Spelling Instruction.* New Jersey: Merrill/Prentice Hall, 1996.

Cunningham, James W., et al. *Middle and Secondary School Reading.* New York: Longman, 1981.

Gifford, Ann P. "Broadening Concepts through Vocabulary Development." *Reading Improvement* (March 2000): 2–12.

Gunning, Thomas G. "Word Building: A Strategic Approach to the Teaching of Phonics." *The Reading Teacher* (March 1995): 484–488.

Nagy, William, et al. "Learning Word Meanings from Context during Normal Reading." *American Education Research Journal* (Summer 1998): 237–270.

Simpson, Phyllis L. Three Step Reading Vocabulary Strategy for Today's Content Area Reading Classroom. *Reading Improvement* (Summer 1996): 76–80.

Sloan, Megan S. "Encouraging Students to Use Interesting Words in their writing." *The Reading Teacher* (November 1996): 268–269.

Zutell, Jerome. "The Directed Spelling Thinking Activity: Providing an Effective Balance in Word Study Instruction." *The Reading Teacher* (October 1996): 98–108.

Web Extensions

<http://www.readwritethink.org/lessons/lesson_view.asp?id=307>
<http://www.readwritethink.org/lessons/lesson_view.asp?id=20>
<http://www.readwritethink.org/lessons/lesson_view.asp?id=773>
<http://www.thinkfinity.org/21stCenturyHome.aspx>
<http://go.hrw.com/ndNSAPI.nd/gohrw_rls1/pKeywordResults?st2%20strategies>
<http://www.readingquest.org/strat/wordmap.html>

Works Cited

Anderson, Richard C., and William E. Nagy. "Word Meanings." In R. Barr, M. L. Kamil, P. B. Mosenthal, & P. D. Pearson (Eds.), *Handbook of Reading Research*, Vol. II. New York: Longman, 1991, pp. 690–724.

Baker, Scott. K., et al. "Vocabulary Acquisition: Research Bases." In D. C. Simmons and E. J. Kame'enui (Eds.), *What Reading Research Tells Us about Children with Diverse Learning Needs*. Mahwah, NJ: Erlbaum, 1998, pp. 183–218.

Blachowitz, Camille I., and Peter J. Fisher. "Vocabulary Instruction." In M. Kamil, P. Mosenthal, P. D. Pearson, and R. Barr (Eds.), *Handbook of Reading Research*, Vol. III. Mahwah, NJ: Erlbaum, 2000, pp. 503–523.

Brett, Arlene, et al. "Vocabulary Acquisition from Listening to Stories and Explanations of Target Words." *Elementary School Journal* (March 1996): 415–422.

Carver, Ronald P., and Robert E. Leibert. "The Effect of Reading Library Books at Different Levels of Difficulty upon Gain in Reading Ability." *Reading Research Quarterly* (January- February-March 1995): 26–47.

Cawelty, George (Ed.). *Handbook of Research on Improving Student Achievement*. 3rd ed. Washington, DC: Educational Research Service, 2004.

Ellis, Edwin S. *The Clarifying Routine*. Kansas: Edge Enterprises, 2002.

Henderson, Ed. *Teaching Spelling*. 2nd ed. Boston: Houghton Mifflin, 1990.

Nagy, William. *Teaching Vocabulary to Improve Reading Comprehension*. Newark, DE: International Reading Association, 1998.

National Reading Panel. *Teaching Children to Read: An Evidence-Based Assessment of the Scientific Research Literature on Reading and Its Implications for Reading Instruction*. Washington, DC: National Institute of Child Health and Human Development, 2000.

Pressley, Michael. "Comprehension Instruction: What Makes Sense Now, What Might Make Sense Soon." *Reading Online*, September 2002,

<http://www.readingonline.org/articles/handbook/pressley/index.htm>.

Rupley, William H., et al. "Vocabulary Instruction in a Balanced Reading Program." *The Reading Teacher* (Dec. 1998-Jan. 1999): 336–346.

Smith, John W., and Warwick B. Elley. *Learning to Read in New Zealand.* Katonah, NY: Richard C. Owen, 1994.

Snow, Catherine E., M. Susan Burns, and Peg Griffin (Eds.). *Preventing Reading Difficulties in Young Children.* Washington, DC: National Academy Press, 1998.

White, Richard T., and Richard R. Gunstone. *Probing Understanding.* New York: Falmer Press, 1992.

9

Frayer Model/Word Sorts

DEFINITION

The Frayer Model of concept development (Frayer, Frederick, and Klausmeier, 1969) is a graphic organizer that is used to help students compare and categorize the essential and nonessential elements of individual words or concepts. Students can see the visual relationship between word analysis and word building by using the Frayer Model. The graphic organizer is a four-square model that requires students to think about words or concepts by defining the term, describing and listing its essential characteristics, providing examples of the word or concept, and providing nonexamples of the word or concept. Highly recommended for visual learners, the Frayer Model is an effective strategy for diverse learners.

Word sorts help students in their ability to recognize semantic relationships among words or concepts. Word sorts require students to categorize words into different categories to discover spelling patterns, meanings, and sound-symbol correspondence (Bear et al., 1996; Schlagal and Schlagal, 1992). There are two types of word sorts: closed sorts and open sorts. When students use a closed word sort, they arrange words into categories that have been determined by the classroom teacher or librarian. Open word sorts, in contrast, allow students the freedom to sort words by developing their own labeled categories. Students are encouraged to find multiple ways to categorize words when using an open word sort. Classifying and reclassifying aids students in their ability to extend and refine their understanding of the vocabulary terms being studied in a particular unit. Because successful Web searching requires students to identify, understand, and use key words to guide their searches for information, this strategy is essential to the information literacy process. Being able to determine the relationships among words helps students gather the data they need; thus, student success depends on search strategy skills as well as the development of a bank of related and relevant words.

RESEARCH FINDINGS

Research indicates that the intentional, explicit teaching of specific words and word-learning strategies can both add words to students' vocabularies (Tomeson and Aarnoutse, 1998; White et al., 1990) and improve reading comprehension of texts containing those words (McKeown, Beck, Omanson, and Pople, 1985).

Graves (2000) notes that if students are to be successful in understanding unfamiliar vocabulary in their reading, they need to learn *about* words, not simply acquire new words.

Students can identify features and examples for a concept after a teacher-led discussion. This activity can be supported with a visual representation (Eeds and Cockrum, 1985).

Students use word sorts to examine and categorize words according to their meaning, graphophonemic clues, similarities, or spelling patterns (Bear et al. 2008).

When used as a categorization activity, word sort helps students develop concepts, improve comprehension, and retain information (Gillett and Temple 1983).

Teaching vocabulary before and after reading benefits the reader (Mealey and Konopak, 1990; Memory, 1990).

STANDARDS

Information Literacy Standards: 1,2,3,6
NCTE/IRA Standards for the English Language Arts: 1,2,4,5,6, 8,9,11,12

STRATEGY NUTS AND BOLTS: IMPLEMENTATION IN THE LIBRARY OR CLASSROOM

Frayer Model

The Frayer Model of concept development is a method of teaching new vocabulary words through direct instruction. It provides a thorough picture of a word by using a graphic organizer and is extremely valuable in teaching complex concepts (Ryder and Graves, 1994), word analysis, and vocabulary building. The Frayer Model is a chart with four sections: definition, characteristics/facts, examples, and non-examples. By using a visual organizer such as the Frayer Model, students develop an understanding of key concepts by drawing on prior knowledge to make connections among concepts while comparing attributes and examples. The strategy also stresses the importance of understanding words in a larger context of reading. Furthermore, students must think critically to find relationships between concepts while making personal associations with the words. Librarians and classroom teachers can use the following simple steps to introduce the Frayer Model to students:

1. The librarian or classroom teacher explains the Frayer Model to students by showing the graphic organizer to the class with an overhead projector or document camera. Alternatively, the teacher can make an example on butcher paper or poster board large enough for the students to see clearly. Using a common word, the librarian or classroom teacher demonstrates the various components of the graphic organizer. It is essential that classroom teacher or librarian model the types and quality of desired answers when modeling the example. Classroom teachers and librarians should allow students to help in the process so that they understand the relationships that exist. Be sure to model appropriate responses to each category.
2. Next, the classroom teacher or librarians selects the list of key concepts or vocabulary terms to be studied either from a reading selection or from a thematic unit of study. Write the list on the chalkboard or overhead projector and review the list with students prior to reading the desired text or beginning the research, depending on the instructional objectives of the lesson or unit.

3. Then, the classroom teacher or librarian divides the students into pairs or small groups. Each pair or small group is assigned a key concept or vocabulary term that they are responsible for defining by using the Frayer Model Graphic Organizer in Figure 9.1. As students read the selection or conduct the research, it is their job to define the term or concept to the best of their ability.
4. Finally, the student pairs or small groups report back to the class by sharing their findings. Students share their answers from each part of the Frayer Model. These reviews allow the class to be exposed to a large number of words. An example of a Frayer Model can be found in Figure 9.2. Words can be added to a word wall, ongoing vocabulary list, or personal dictionary.

Word Sorts

According to Harris (2007), middle and high school teachers are not fully prepared to teach students word identification strategies since it is assumed that adolescents develop, and many times master, this skill before entering high school. At the very least, students must possess a basic proficiency in word identification. Word sorts represent one strategy that can give students the tools to deal effectively with unfamiliar vocabulary. They can be used in large-group or small-group settings. "All word sorts follow the same basic procedure: *demonstration, sort and check, reflect,* and *declare*" (Harris, 2007). The purpose of word sorts is to help students focus on conceptual and/or phonological features of words. Students sort words based on prior experience. This strategy can promote students' critical thinking and enable them to consider how words are related to each other. The following steps can be used by the classroom teacher or librarian when preparing word sorts for students:

1. The classroom teacher or librarian selects words for study on the basis of the current curriculum content being taught or other learning objectives. The librarian may want to consult the classroom teacher for suggestions on words that may be troubling for students or that must become part of a unit of study. Typically, teachers or librarians select words that are related in some way and have commonalities in inflectional endings or other features.

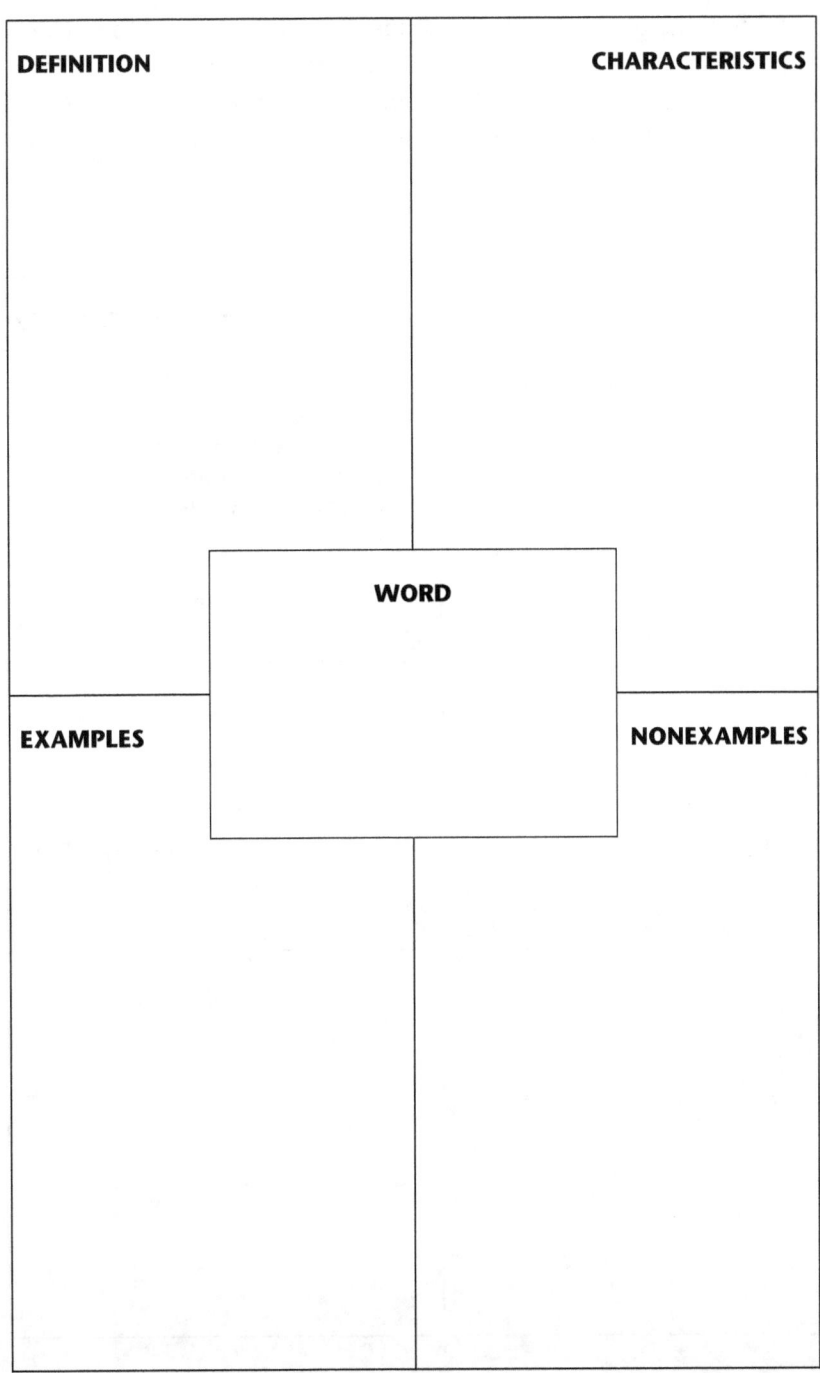

FIGURE 9.1: Frayer Model Graphic Organizer

In the center of the graphic organizer, students record the word to research. In the upper left corner, the student should define the word that is pertinent and essential to the unit of study. For examples and nonexamples, students should draw properly formed cumulonimbus clouds and non-cumulonimbus clouds.

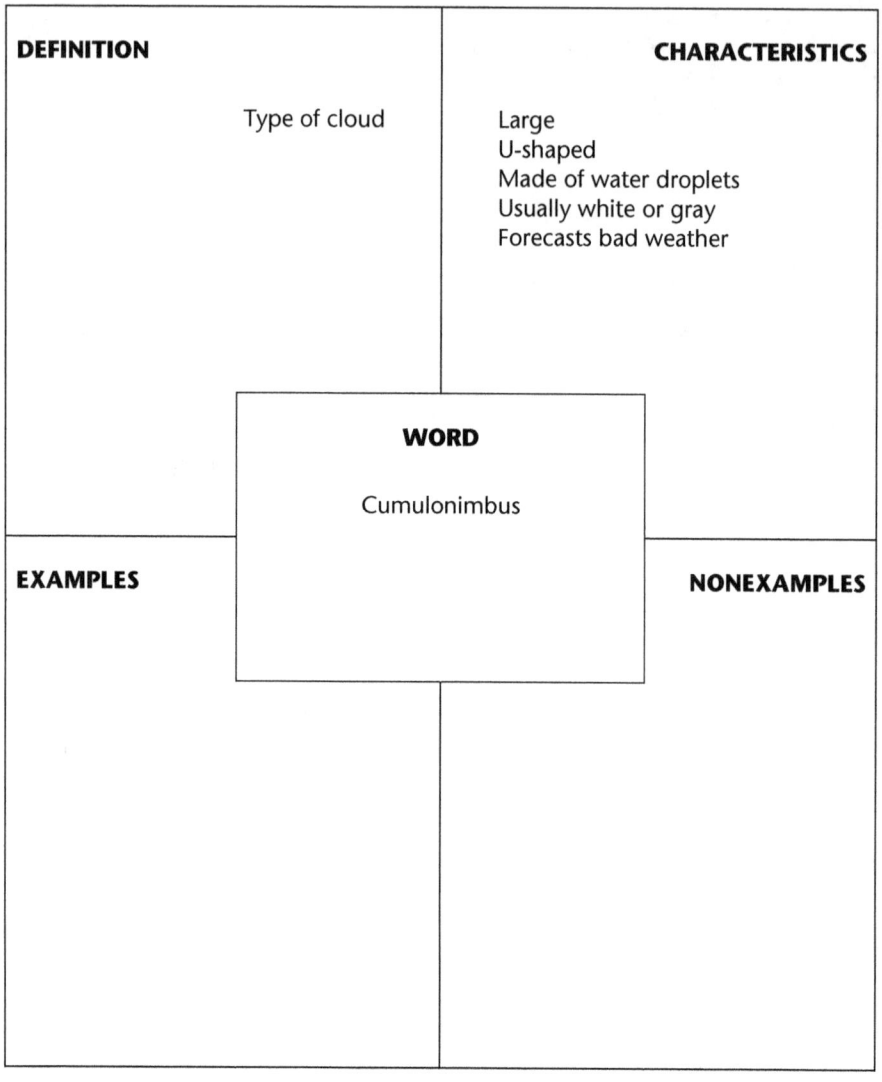

FIGURE 9.2: Frayer Model Example

2. Next, the classroom teacher or librarian decides if students will take part in an open or closed word sort. Open word sorts give students the freedom to determine categories for words they are sorting, while closed word sorts allow the instructor to predetermine the categories for such words. Students can sort words and word parts into columns according to part of speech, word history and origins, and/or prefix, suffix, and word part.
3. Then, the classroom teacher or librarian compiles and prepares the list of words that represent the unit of study. The words can then be typed onto 3 x 5 inch index cards for manipulation purposes. An alternative is to prepare a graph with columns for sorting.
4. The students then physically categorize the words, making a record of their categories. The permanent record can be completed in many different ways. For instance, students may choose to glue cards to butcher paper and display the resulting chart in the classroom or library for future use and reference, or they may decide to categorize words by typing them using a word processing program. Finally, students or small groups may decide to record their words using the Word Sort Organizer in Figure 9.3.

In sum, it is imperative that students be given time to share word sorts with classmates, articulating the categories used (open word sort). By hearing classmates' thought processes, students learn how others have categorized words, enabling them to make additional connections to improve their understanding.

This strategy can be easily adapted to meet a variety of students' needs. Vocabulary skills are a critical component that allows students access to proficient reading. Furthermore, word sorts give struggling readers support through scaffolding (closed words sorts) while allowing opportunities for students to make choices (open word sorts). This versatile strategy has great potential to introduce students to words that they can eventually use proficiently in reading, writing, and speaking. When word sorts are used in a small- or whole-group format, the conversation among group members is almost as important to the learning experience as the placement of the cards, because students must defend their reasoning for word placements. If one

Word Sort for _____

Topic				
Vocabulary				

FIGURE 9.3: Word Sort Organizer

student questions another's placement, the discussion will further this effect. Any dissent will result in students referencing their notes and text for more information. This defining and clarifying process assists students in developing the information literacy skills of critically examining, analyzing, and evaluating word placements. The strategy also assists students in reflecting, rethinking, and narrowing or broadening the terms used to perform a productive Web search process and in developing effective questions to guide their research.

EXTENDING THE STRATEGY FOR DIVERSE LEARNERS AND STUDENTS WITH SPECIAL NEEDS

Classroom teachers and librarians may find that both the Frayer Model and Word Sorts are excellent strategies to use with English language learners and students with special needs because of the accessibility of both strategies. Both strategies can be easily integrated into classroom and library media centers. The Frayer Model can be adapted by allowing students to draw pictures instead of using words. For many ELL and special needs students, this strategy can provide support and flexibility. Heterogeneously grouping students to work in pairs or small groups provides verbal opportunities for students. English language learners and special-needs students can benefit from the interaction that cooperative learning provides.

Word Sorts can be adapted likewise for ELL and special-needs students. Closed word sorts may provide the guidance such students need when categorizing words independently, and open word sorts give students freedom to create categories of their own. By categorizing according to common attributes, students can easily see the connections between and among words. Common attributes may include inflectional endings, prefixes, suffixes, root words, or any common feature of the chosen words. Additionally, classroom teachers and librarians can encourage students to use organizers as references. Classroom teachers may want to consider allowing students to use graphic organizers on assessments measures as adaptations.

Another variation to consider is to push back the desks or tables and to complete the words sorts on the floor, in the hallway, or in some other large space. Word association games can be another technique to use with ELL students and students with special needs.

COLLABORATIVE CONNECTIONS

It is imperative that the classroom teacher and librarian collaborate on when and how to use either the Frayer Model or Word Sorts in their respective locales. Librarians may want to conference with the classroom teacher to find out what vocabulary terms need extra attention in the library. Likewise, the librarian may find that students need additional work on specific or specialized vocabulary.

ASSESSMENT TOOLS

The classroom teacher and the librarian can develop inquiry questions on the topic of study. They can have students identify the key words and key concepts in the question. They can also instruct students to create a Keyword Search Expansion Chart like the one shown in Figure 9.4 to test the list of words/concepts to locate information or useful sources on the Web related to the topic of study and have the students record their findings on the chart.

Where Can I Learn More about Frayer Model/Word Sorts?

Bear, Donald R., et al. *Words Their Way: Word Study for Phonics, Vocabulary, and Spelling Instruction*. Upper Saddle River, NJ: Merrill/Prentice Hall, 1996.

Cunningham, Pam M. *Phonics They Use: Words for Reading and Writing*. 4th ed. New York: Harper Collins, 2005.

Johns, Jerry, and Roberta Berglund. *Strategies for Content Area Learning*. Dubuque, IA: Kendall/Hunt, 2002.

Vacca, Richard T., and Jo Anne L. Vacca. *Content Area Reading: Literacy and Learning across the Curriculum*. New York: Addison-Wesley, 1999.

Wagstaff, Janiel M. *Teaching Reading and Writing with Word Walls*. New York: Scholastic, 1999.

Web Extensions

<http:www.edu.place.com/rdg/hmsv/8/letterwordcards/p004-5.pdf>
<http://www.readwritethink.org/lessons/lesson_view.asp?id=795>
<http://wvde.state.wv.us/strategybank/FrayerModel.html>
<http://www.justreadnow.com/strategies/frayer.htm>
<http://its.guilford.k12.nc.us/act/strategies/Frayer.htm>
<http://www.adlit.org/strategies/22369>

Key Word, Phrase, Concept	Expansion	Number of Searches	Effective Search Term? Yes/No

FIGURE 9.4: Keyword Search Expansion Chart

Works Cited

Bear, Donald R., et al. *Words Their Way: Word Study for Phonics, Vocabulary, and Spelling Instruction.* Upper Saddle River, NJ: Merrill/Prentice Hall, 2008.

Eeds, Maryanne, and Ward A. Cockrum. A. "Teaching Word Meanings by Expanding Schemata vs. Dictionary Work vs. Reading in Context." *Journal of Reading* (March 1985): 492–497.

Frayer, Dorothy A. *A Schema for Testing the Level of Cognitive Mastery.* Madison: Wisconsin Center for Education Research, 1969.

Gillett, Jean W., and Charles Temple. *Understanding Reading Problems: Assessment and instruction.* Boston: Little, Brown, 1983.

Graves, Michael. F. "A Vocabulary Program to Complement and Bolster a Middle-Grade Comprehension Program." In B.M. Taylor, M.F. Graves, and P. van den Broek (Eds.), *Reading for Meaning: Fostering Comprehension in the Middle Grades.* New York: Teachers College Press; Newark, DE: International Reading Association, 2000, pp. 116–135.

Harris, Linsay, A. "Adolescent Literacy: Wordy Study with Middle and High School Students." *Teaching Exceptional Children Plus* (March 2007): 4.

McKeown, Margaret G., et al. "Some Effects of the Nature and Frequency of Vocabulary Instruction on the Knowledge and Use of Words." *Reading Research Quarterly* (Fall 1985): 522–535.

Mealey, Donna, and Bonnie Konopak. "Content Area Vocabulary Instruction: Is Preteaching Worth the Effort?" *Reading Exploration and Discovery* (Fall 1990): 39–42.

Memory, David M. "Teaching Technical Vocabulary: Before, during, or after Reading Assignments." *Journal of Reading Behavior* (March 1990): 39–53.

Ryder, Randall J., and Michael F. Graves. *Reading and Learning in the Content Areas.* 2nd ed. New York: Merrill, 1994.

Schlagal, Robert C., and Joy Harris Schlagal. "The Integral Character of Spelling: Teaching Strategies for Multiple Purposes." *Language Arts* (October 1992): 418–424.

Tomeson, Marieke, and Cor Aarnoutse. "Effects of an Instructional Programme for Deriving Word Meanings." *Educational Studies* (April 1998): 107–128.

White, Thomas G., et al. "Teaching Elementary Students to Use Word-Part Clues." *The Reading Teacher* (January 1989): 302–309.

APPENDIX

Collaboration: Web 2.0

A NOTE ON NEW PARTICIPATORY RESOURCES

In the previous chapters, the authors discussed a number of emerging technologies, such as blogs, wikis, hyperlinked journals, and podcasts, as tools to promote reading in the content areas. We wanted to include a separate section to discuss a few more of the 21st-century literacies for the new Read/Write Web for several reasons. First, the authors believe that emerging technologies are modifying the relationships between teachers and students, making quality teaching more complex and more difficult in some cases. Second, it is our belief that student communities play an important role in the teaching process. Third, although faculty members are equally engaged in the teaching and the learning processes, their willingness to explore and adopt participatory technology that will transform their teaching may vary according to their philosophy. Fourth, school districts' infrastructure to support technology-enhanced instruction is diverse and varies widely across school districts. Thus, we have written this special section devoted to a few of the emerging technologies or new "cool tools" to challenge teachers to think differently about their classrooms and to form collaborative partnerships with the librarian to weave the new interactive Web into their practice. The tools of the new Internet provide opportunities for collaboration and for constructive learning and allow students to become meaningful contributors to the vast body of knowledge available on the Internet in addition to promoting literacy skills.

This special section is divided into two parts, a Web 2.0 glossary and a Webliography of reading and vocabulary Web publishing and information-gathering tools. It is the authors' hope that these sections will assist both teachers and librarians as they move from the traditional memorizing of facts and formulas and other "closed" sources of information, such as textbooks, to transforming their teaching to invite students to become active participants in the creation of information.

To begin with, we thought classroom teachers and librarians would find the following Web 2.0 glossary useful as a springboard to begin conversations about the new Read/Write Web tools in the content of good literacy instruction. Each of these Web tools is a powerful device in its own right; not only do these tools transform teaching, but they also motivate and update students' reading and research skills. Working in collaboration, the classroom teacher and the librarian can design lessons to integrate these tools into the curriculum.

WEB 2.0 GLOSSARY

43 Things—A social networking site based on the principles of tagging, where users create a list of things they would like to do or goals they would like to accomplish. Items on this list are then matched with similar items on other people's lists. This concept is a type of folksonomy. <http://www.43things.com>

Ajax (Asynchronous JavaScript and XML)—A Web development technique used to increase the speed, usability, and interactivity of a Web page.

Blog—A user-generated Web site where the user shares his or her ideas about events or some topic.

del.icio.us—A social bookmarking Web site where users tag their bookmarks with keywords of their choosing. The site allows users to share what they have bookmarked and to see the links others have bookmarked <http//:del.icio.us/>

Digg—Users submit science- and technology-based news stories and Web sites that are then promoted to the front page through a user ranking system. This site combines social bookmarking, blogging, and syndication with nonhierarchical, democratic editorial control. <http://www.digg.com/>

Facebook—A social networking site where people can choose to join any number of participating networks based on topics such as profession, schools attended, or interests. <www.facebook.com>

Flickr—A photosharing Web site that allows photos to be tagged and browsed by folksonic means. <http://www.flickr.com>

Folksonomy—A system that allows users to generate their own taxonomies to categorize and retrieve information on the Internet through the process of tagging. Ideally, this allows for information sharing between users with a similar conceptual framework of terms.

Furl—(File Uniform Resource Locators) a social bookmarking Web site that allows its members to store and search copies of Web pages categorized by topics. <http://furl.net>

The Long Tail—A phrase purportedly coined by Chris Anderson to describe a relative handful of Weblogs that have many links to them, but "the long tail" of most Weblogs may only have a handful of links to them.

MySpace—An international social networking Web site where users submit their own pages, which includes a personal profile, a network of friends, blogs, groups, photos, music, and videos. <http://www.myspace.com>

Pandora—An Internet radio service created by the Music Genome Project that recommends music to its users by playing selections that are musically similar to songs or artists that users enter. <http://www.pandora.com/>

Podcasting—The method by which a specific type of Webcast is syndicated.

There are several uses of podcasting in education: (1) to share information at any time between students and teachers; (2) to communicate with parents and community; (3) to record lessons; and (4) to publish student presentations.

RSS (Really Simple Syndication, Rich Site Summary, or RDF Site Summary)—Family of Web feed formats used to publish frequently updated content, such as blogs, news feeds, or podcasts.

Second Life—A virtual social networking world where users called "Residents" can explore, meet other residents, socialize, and create and trade virtual property and services. <http://secondlife.com/#>

Semantic Web—Extension of the World Wide Web where Web content can be expressed in a form that can be read and used by software agents, in addition to natural language. This allows users to find, share, and integrate information more easily.

Skype—A peer-to-peer Internet network that allows for free voice and video conferencing, decentralized technology to overcome common firewall and network address problems, and countermeasures against reverse engineering of the software. <http://www.skype.com/>

SlideShare—A free service for sharing presentations and slideshows. <http://www.slideshare.net>

Social bookmarking—Web sites that allow their users to store, classify, and share search links through the use of folksonomy techniques.

Social Network—Social structure made up of nodes (individuals within networks) and ties (relationship between the individuals).

Social Software—Modes of computer-mediated communication that result in "community formation" either online or in person.

Tagging—A relevant keyword or words assigned to a piece of information, such as a picture or article, usually chosen informally by the creator of the item. This allows for a flexible taxonomy that helps readers to quickly locate all pages associated with the assigned term.

Technorati—Internet search engine for searching blogs that competes with Google and Yahoo. <http://www.technorati.com/>

Twitter—Social networking Web site where users can send text-based posts through SMS (Short Message Service), instant messaging, the Twitter Web site, or an application such as Twitterrific. These posts are displayed on the users' profile page and also are instantly delivered to other users who are signed up to receive them. <http://www.twitter.com>

Weblogs—the most widely adopted tool of the Read/Write Web, which can take many forms; students can write about personal reactions to topics covered in class, post links, write reflectively, and summarize or annotate reading.

Wiki—A Web site that permits users to add, remove, and edit content without registering, allowing for mass collaborative authoring.

Wikipedia—A type of encyclopedic wiki written collaboratively by volunteers and edited by anyone with access. <http://www.wikipedia.org/>

YouTube—Video-sharing Web site where users can upload, view, and share video clips. <http://www.youtube.com/>

Zude—A social Webpage network used specifically for creating personalized webpages. <http://www.zude.com>

The authors have selected the following Web sites to foster sound social learning connections to develop reading, vocabulary, writing, and information literacy skills.

READING

Mr. William Shakespeare and the Internet

<http://daphne.palomar.edu/Shakespeare>

Teach Shakespeare electronically using this link, which provides an annotated set of links Click on "Educational" in the frame on the left and you get to a three-page list of how-to-teach sites. Complete with RSS feeds.

Larry Ferlazzo's Best Websites to Help Beginning Readers

<http://larryferlazzo.edublogs.org/2008/01/22/the-best-websites-to-help-beginning-readers/>

This site is especially good for working with students with special needs and ELL students.

Tom Robb Reading List

<http://www.kyoto-su.ac.jp/~trobb/read/read.html>

This site contains a list of materials that can be used for lower-level reading classes at this URL.

The Case

<http://www.TheCase.com/>

The Case is dedicated to mystery lovers. Sign up to have short little mysteries sent to your e-mail account each week. Each one is a situational puzzle with clues and a small number of questions that cause you to search the little story for the clues.

There are more mysteries under that category at the Tower of English: <http://towerofenglish.com/>.

Extensive Reading

<http://www.extensivereading.net/index.html>

A Web site dedicated to exploring all aspects of the Extensive Reading (ER) Approach, this site contains a large annotated bibliography of works on ER, information on how to start your own ER program, information on resources for ER such as graded readers, and even an interactive chat page for your questions and advice.

Takako's Great Adventure

<http://international.ouc.bc.ca/takako/>

This is a useful site for struggling readers who can scroll the text of a Takako novel online while listening to MP3 recordings.

The Moonlit Road

<http://www.themoonlitroad.com/>

Especially good for ELL, these interactive ghost stories and strange folktales of the American South are told by the region's most celebrated storytellers.

TrackStar

<http://scrtec.org/track/>

Developed at the University of Kansas, this is a free, online tool for making exercises from pages on the Web. Make your own activity, make a quiz for your exercise, make a Webpage from a template to be a part of the Web activity, or search the hundreds of previously made "tracks" and modify one to suit your purposes.

Script-O! Quiz Maker

<http://www.readingmatrix.com/quizmaker/index.php>

This tool allows teachers to create online learning activities based on their own classroom materials. Teachers and librarians can create online quizzes in a variety of formats and publish them on the Web. Add your own Web links, password protect quizzes, provide immediate feedback, and download scores in just a few easy steps

VOCABULARY

Vocabulary

<http://www.voycabulary.com/>

The site allows you to enter a word. The word then becomes hot-linked to a dictionary or thesaurus.

Word Dragon

<http://www.sccd.ctc.edu/~ssesl/puzzlelinks.html>

This site is designed for scrambled word/sentence exercises.

Quizlet

<http://www.call-is.org.>

Provide a word list, and this tool generates exercises that can be done in collaboration with other learners.

Reading/Vocabulary Lessons

<http://www.cup.cam.ac.uk/elt/newibe/txtintro.html>

This site contains a series of reading lessons, each of which has one large frame on the top with a reading text and two small frames on the bottom that display comprehension questions and answers or the definitions of words in the text that the reader doesn't understand.

INDEX

A

American Association of School Librarians Standards for the 21st Century Learner. *See* Standards
Anticipation guides, 35–42

F

Frayer model, 87–98

I

Information Literacy Standards for Student Learning. *See* Standards
International Reading Association Standards for English Language Arts. *See* Standards

N

National Council For Teachers of English Standards for the English Language Arts. *See* Standards
NCTE/IRA Standards for English Language Arts. *See* Standards

Q

Question-answer relationships, 3–15
Questioning the author, 43–54

R

Reciprocal teaching, 26–32

S

Semantic feature analysis, 68–75
SQ3R. *See* Survey, question, read, recite, review
Standards for English Language Arts. *See* Standards
Standards: Information Literacy Standards for

Standards (*continued*)
    Student Learning, xxiii, xxiv, xxv; NCTE/IRA Standards for English Language Arts, xxi, xxiii, xxiv; Standards for the 21st Century Learner, xvii, xix, xxi
Survey, question, read, recite, review, 55–63

T

Think alouds, 17–25

W

Web 2.0, 99–102
Word journals, 76–86
Word questioning maps, 76–86
Word sorts, 87–98

www.ingramcontent.com/pod-product-compliance
Lightning Source LLC
Chambersburg PA
CBHW070627300426
44113CB00010B/1684